Quilted Faces

An Introduction to Fabric Portraits

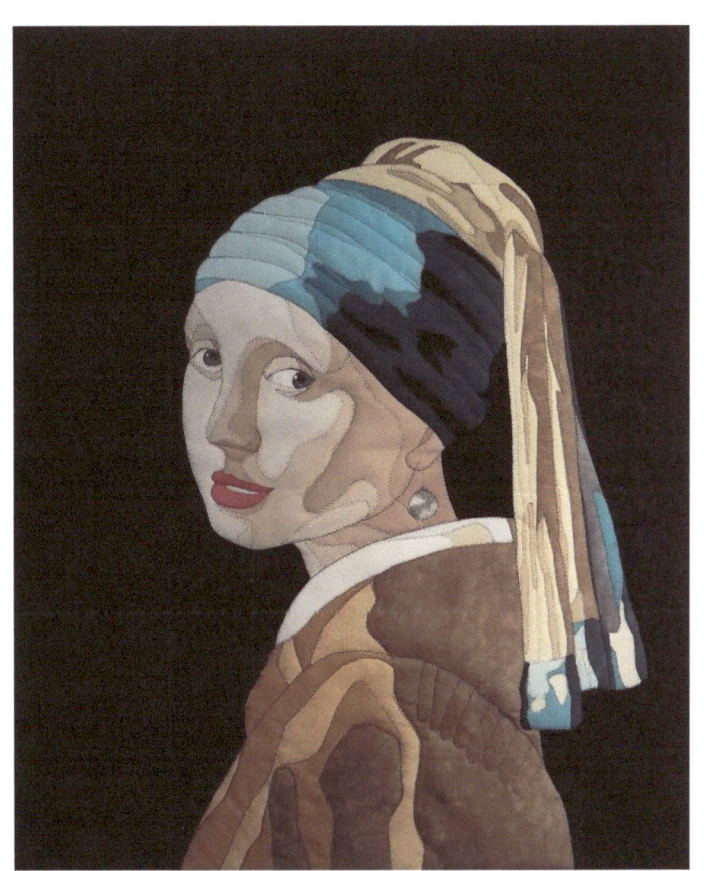

Valerie Wilson

Copyright © 2020 Valerie Wilson

All rights reserved. No portion of this book may be reproduced, stored in a retrieval system, or transmitted in any form or by any means; electronic, mechanical, photocopy, recording, scanning, or other, except for brief quotations in critical reviews or articles, without the prior written permission of the author or publisher.

Publisher: RoseDale Publishing

Editing: Clara Rose & Company

ISBN: 978-1-7344263-6-6

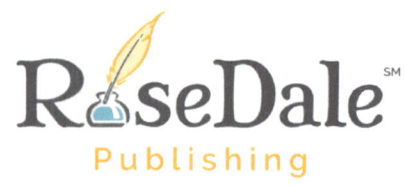

Dedication

To my wonderful husband Bob for believing
in me and being so supportive of my art career.

Table of Contents

Dedication	iii
Acknowledgments	vii
Foreword	ix
Chapter 1 - Getting Started	5
Chapter 2 - Understanding Values	17
Chapter 3 - Choosing Your Fabrics	31
Chapter 4 - Creating Your Portrait	41
Chapter 5 - Reviewing Your Work and Fusing	59
Chapter 6 - Stitching and Adding Detail	71
Chapter 7 - Quilting Your Portrait	81
Chapter 8 - Finishing Touches	89
Letter From The Author	103
Your Resources	105
Pattern For This Project	107

Acknowledgments

Many thanks to Clara Rose, my editor, for encouraging me and providing so much support throughout the process of writing and publishing this book. And for being my tester trying out the instructions.

To all those enthusiastic students who have taken my courses and taught me so much too!

Thank you to all those people who love creating fabric portraits and your encouragement to write this book.

To my fibre art group, the Fibre Art Divas, for all your enthusiasm and abundant creativity and your belief in me.

My Business Support group who believed I could write a book and all their support and encouragement.

Foreword

I have known Val Wilson for over a decade and often been up to my elbows with fabric dyeing and flour resist paste in her studio. Oh, how she had the patience to put up with me, I have no idea. As an author myself and the host of the Quilter on Fire podcast, I know the work that goes into writing about your passion and I am honoured to be the one she chose to write this foreword.

As her fibre art friend, over the years I have watched her skill for creating photo to fibre art pieces continuously grow. The joy in her portrait explorations has not only remained constant but has absolutely consumed her with a passion. She shares a wonderful sense of history in her portrait choices and has shown her fibre art in galleries and quilt shows across Canada and around the world. This book is the perfect mix of technique and inspiration and was a natural next step after her popular online fabric portraits course.

I had the joy of working with Val on a Fibre Art Network challenge several years ago. We had to partner up and one quilter (Val) was to make a fabric portrait and her challenge partner (me) was to make an abstract version of that art piece. I was so impressed with the vibrant colour palette, intricate detail of the cut appliqué, and the incredible stitching on her 1950's car portrait, that it was easy to be inspired to create a partner piece. Working with her was a breeze and it was one of my favourite challenges to this day.

When her quilt "A French Wonder" was featured on the cover of the Quilt Canada Show Guide I was not in the least bit surprised. When Val creates intricately detailed fabric portraits of people from the past, she breathes new life into grey and forgotten photos of ordinary people.

This book features Val's fibre art piece - "Girl With a Pearl Earring" as the learning centrepiece and takes you from the tools you need through the creation process start to finish. She demonstrates a wide variety of techniques and has a knack for getting her students past the fear of choosing colour values. Val has put years of trial and error and a whole lot of heart into the making of this book.

When you work through the pages you will discover your own passion for portraits in fibre art and you just may become hooked for years to come.

Brandy Maslowski

Brandy Maslowski brings more joy and less overwhelm to quilters from her home studio in Summerland, BC, Canada. You can find her everywhere online as the Quilter on Fire.

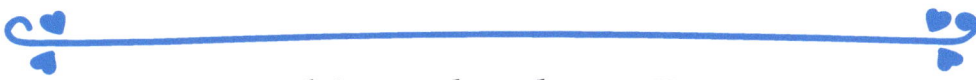

This Book Belongs To

"Don't limit your challenges.
Challenge your limits."
– Jerry Dunn

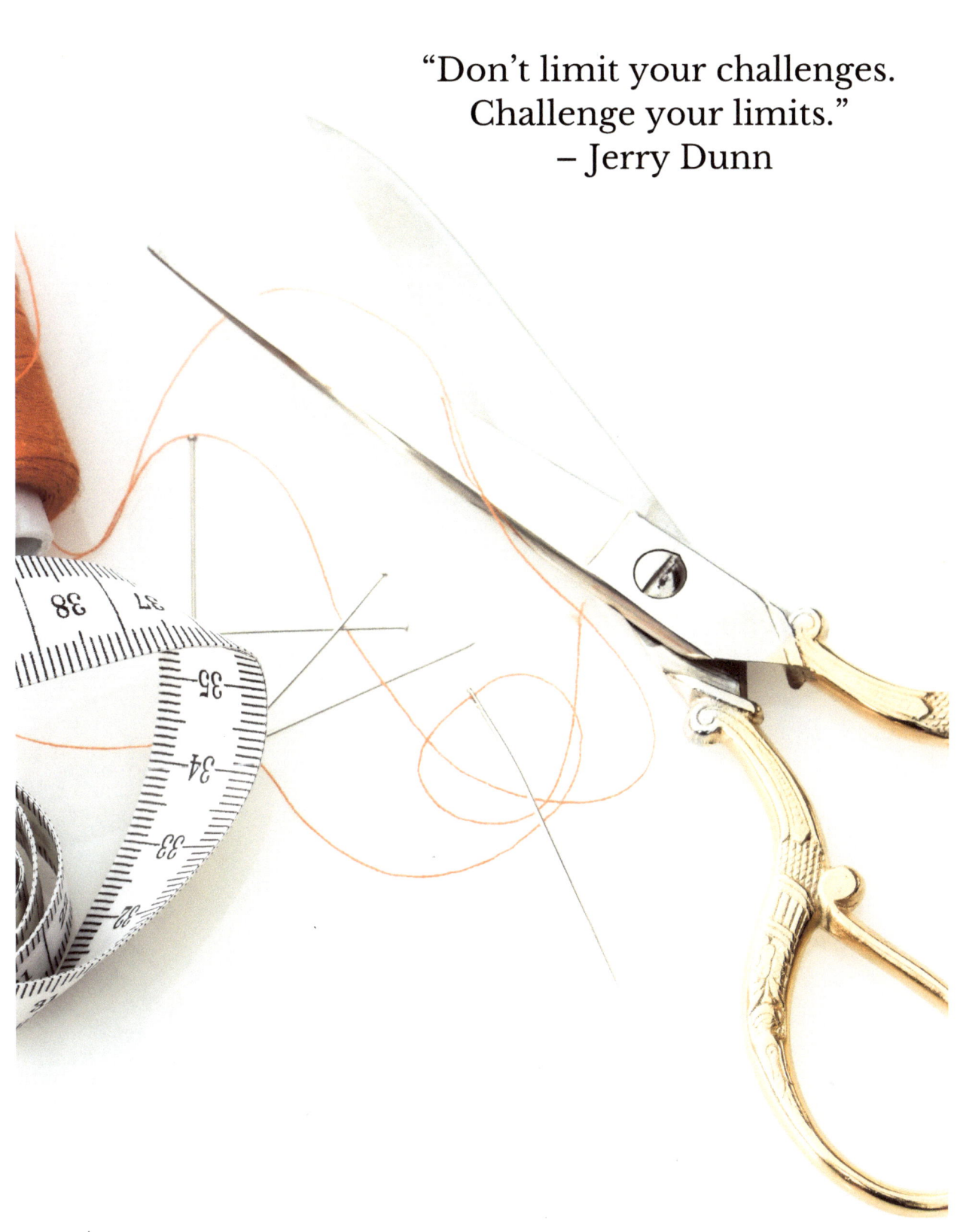

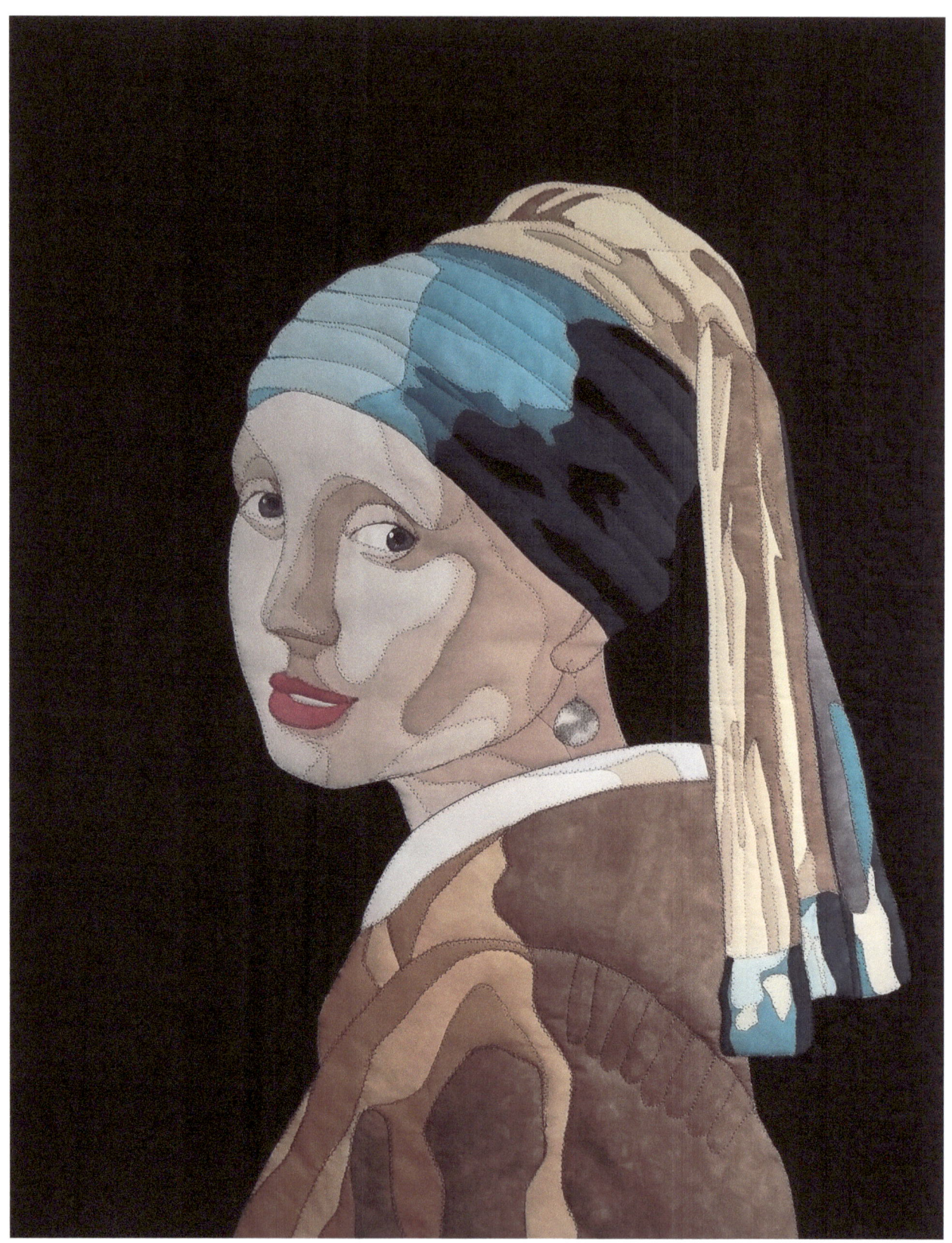

Chapter 1
Getting Started

Welcome to the world of fabric portraits!

Creating a likeness of a person in fabric is very rewarding, as you see them come to life in your quilt. I have been creating portraits in fabric since 2010, I liken my process to that of puzzle making, except here, we create the puzzle, and then fit all the pieces together.

I have been teaching classes for many years, and often students will ask me if I have a book they could buy. In response, I wanted to write a book which would give quilters a taste of what creating a fabric portrait is all about.

Students are often afraid of trying faces, they worry it won't look like the person they are trying to represent. So, I developed the Introduction to Portraits class. This book brings that course to you.

It is designed to help you get over the fear of starting a portrait in fabric. You will be provided with a pattern to follow and a step by step process for creating a likeness of the painting, The Girl with the Pearl Earring.

Working through this book will help you to develop your confidence and build the skills needed to take the next step, which is creating your personalized portrait.

My advanced course (details in the Resources section) teaches you how to work from your photo, edit that photo and create your pattern, as well as take you step by step through the process of creating your heirloom portrait.

For now, the focus will be on creating The Girl with the Pearl Earring portrait as seen here.

In this first chapter, you will find a detailed supply list and instructions on how to use the included pattern, to start creating your first portrait.

Organizing your Tools and Supplies

Check your supplies and see which of the items you already have. Then make a list of the items you still need and either purchase or borrow them.

You can order supplies from my store: artisticquilts.net There is a beginner kit available that includes face fabric and essential tools.

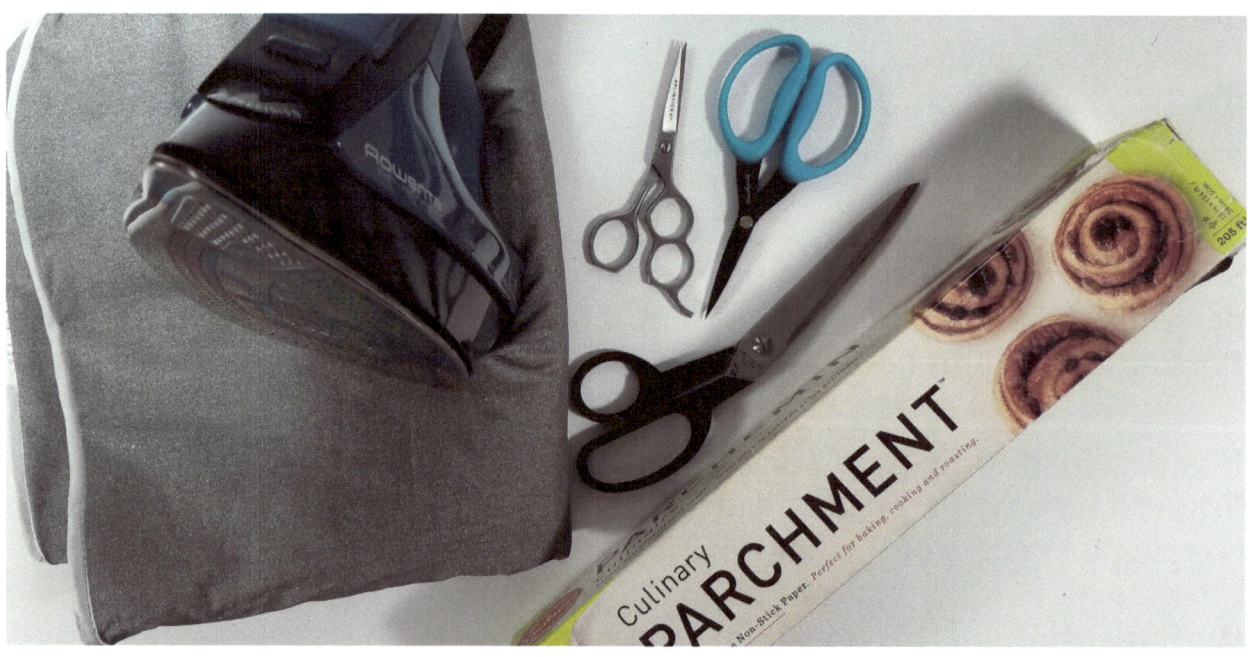

Basic Equipment for sewing, cutting, and fusing

- *Sharp fabric scissors*
- *Paper scissors*
- *Iron and ironing board*
- *Non-stick sheet (for use when fusing the fabric or you can use parchment paper)*
- *Sewing machine, preferably with a zigzag stitch setting*

Supplies - Creating and Enlarging the Pattern

- Access to a photocopier - optional (see the section on enlarging your pattern)

- Computer (or access to one)

- Matte finish scotch tape (for taping your pattern pages together when you print them)

Clear Mylar (Dura-Lar) approx. 18" x 24" - the .003 thickness is fine. You can use a thinner thickness if so desired. The advantage to using the Mylar is the Sharpie lines will erase completely, whereas it can leave shadow marks on regular plastic.

An alternative would be clear plastic – approximately 18" x 24". You will be using this for your design, so you want a slightly heavier plastic, like a piece of plastic tablecloth, plastic tablecloth protector, or shower curtain liner. Try the dollar stores for this item. Fabric stores often sell plastic by the yard.

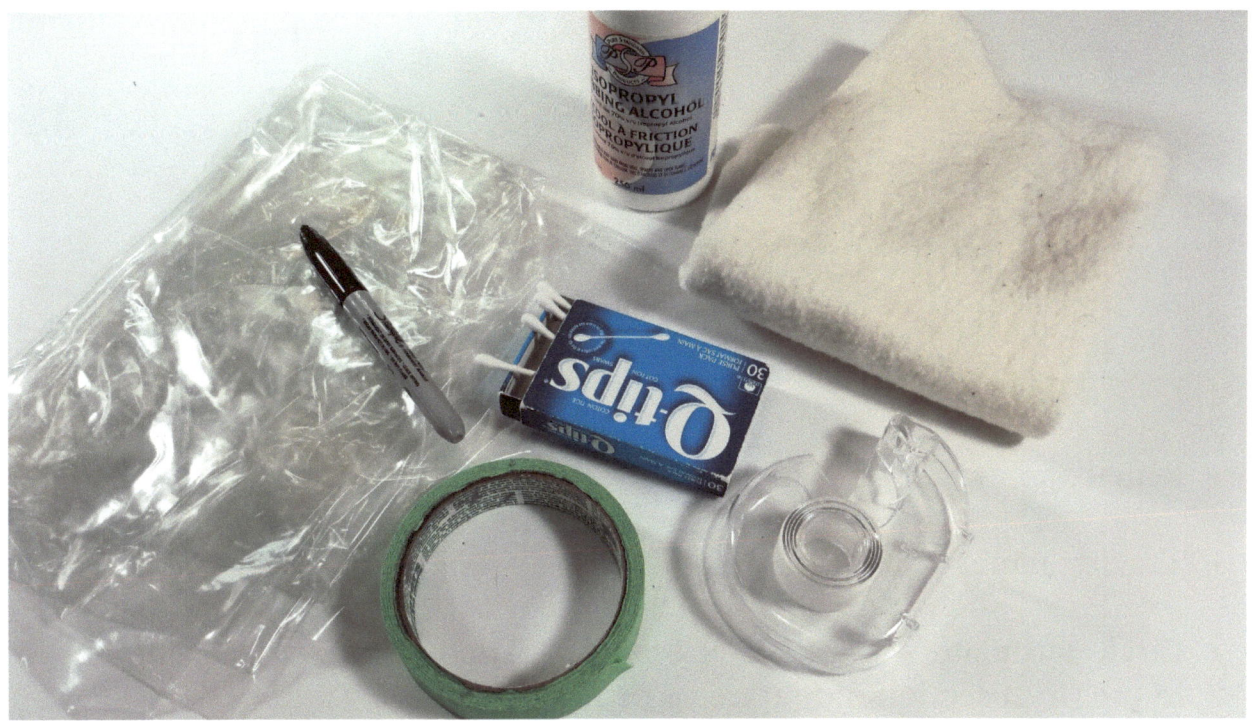

- Painters tape or masking tape.

- Sharpie marker Fine point – black. The Ultrafine tip is too fine!

- Rubbing alcohol (can be found at the drug store) – used for removing the Sharpie from the Mylar or plastic

- Cotton tipped swabs or makeup remover pads– used with the rubbing alcohol for removing Sharpie from the plastic if you make mistakes in tracing your pattern.

Supplies used in Creating your Portrait

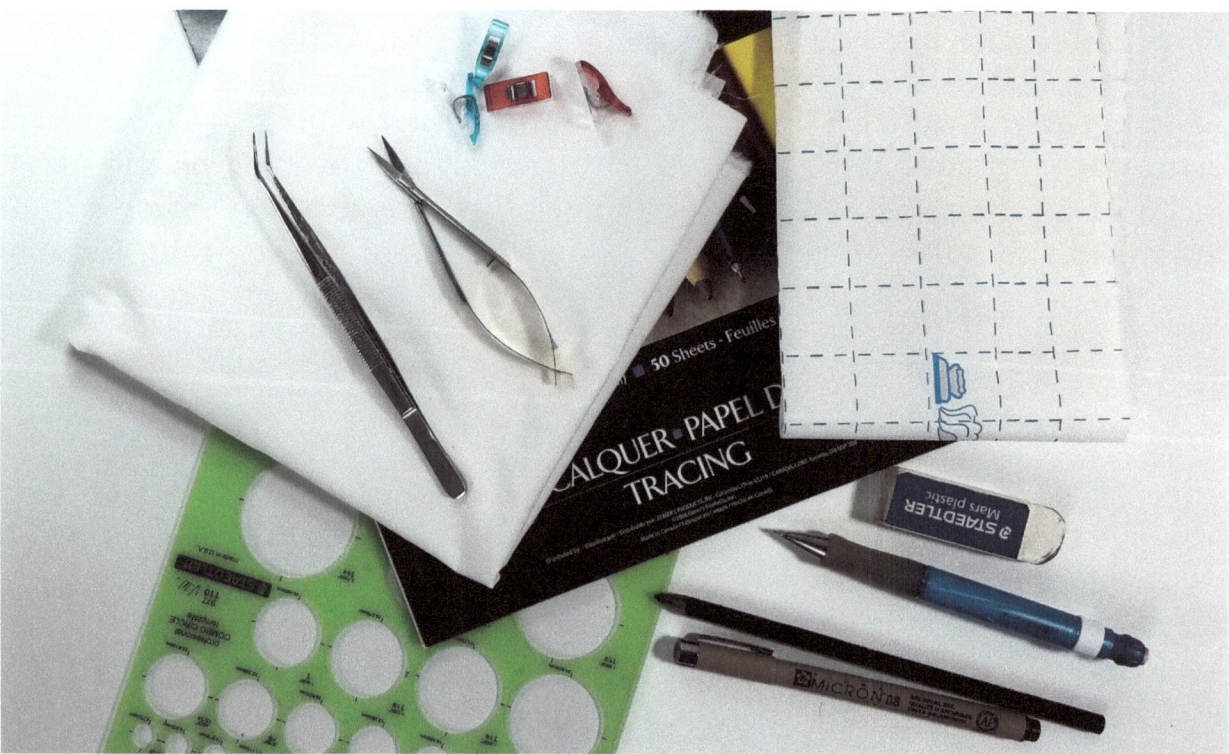

- Pencil and eraser

- Tracing paper

- Circle template – available at Staples - These templates can be found in the Craft section of Staples or ordered online.

- Foam core (sometimes called foam board) large enough for your portrait (available at Staples, Wal-Mart or Michaels). The 18" x 24" size is good. And the ¼" thick is OK too. This will be used as a portable design wall.

- White fabric (for a foundation to work on) large enough for your portrait. Suggest 18" x 24". I recommend prewashing and ironing your fabric so that the fusible will stick to it easily. The fabric can be cotton or cotton/poly blend but should be a smooth weave fabric.

- Fusible - Lite Steam-A-Seam 2® This fusible has 2 sticky sides to it which is helpful for this technique as you can place your pieces on your design wall and they will stay in place. Another benefit is that the pieces are easily adjusted in position or removed and replaced.

If you can find Lite Steam-A-Seam 2® on a roll, purchase a yard or two. In my classes, we have found some issues with the packaged sheets not being sticky enough.

NOTE: Other fusible products can be used, but then you will need a bunch of pins to hold pieces in place until you can fuse them. If you use short applique pins, you can poke the pins into the foam core to hold the fabric pieces in place.

- Wonder clips or similar binding clips. Several companies now make this kind of clip, you will only need 5 or 6 of them. Get the smaller clips, not the long ones.

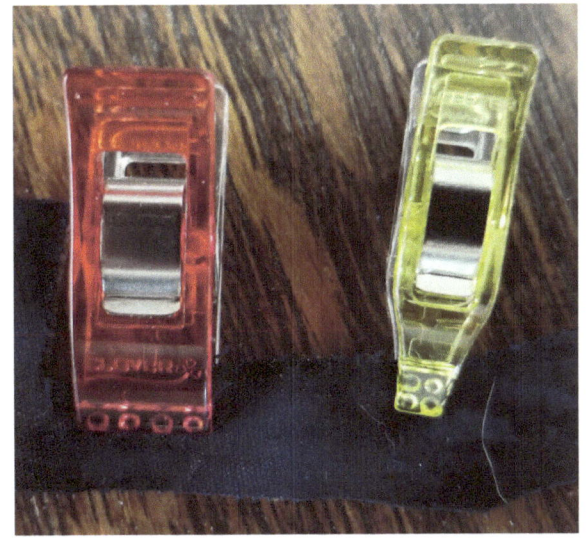

These are a necessity as the Lite Steam-A-Seam 2® leaves a sticky residue on straight pins, which then if used with light fabrics, leave black glue marks by the pinholes.

- Fine curved tip snips are very handy to have. I use them for trimming fine stray threads off the edges of the fabric pieces once they have been fused in place.

- Coloured pencil in black.

- Tweezers (very useful for placing small pieces of fabric). Fine tip, long-handled ones are the best, as they slip easily under the edges of the fabric and the plastic overlay.

- Pigma pen (sometimes called a Pigma brush pen, in some art supply stores) 08 size. Available from my store as well: artisticquilts.net

- Fabric for the portrait – detailed in Chapter 3, but read Chapter 2 first before selecting your fabrics.

- Batting – the type is your personal choice. I will be discussing batting more in Chapter 8 but note the Pro tip below for sizing.

Pro Tip: The quilt backing and batting both need to be larger than the quilt top by about 2-3 inches on all sides. This extra room allows for "shrinkage" as the quilt is quilted. The quilting tends to pull in the quilt a bit and can distort the edges. Having the batting and backing larger allows some wiggle room for squaring up after the quilting has been completed.

Using a Design Wall

A design wall is a very useful tool. We view portraits at eye level most of the time and your quilt will hang on a wall, so it is important to check that perspective.

By having your work up vertically vs. down on a table, you are easily able to see what is working and what isn't. The foam core in the supply list is meant to be your design wall. It is very lightweight and you can easily move it around if needed.

Find a place to prop the foam core up if possible. If your only option is to work flat, be sure to place the design wall up vertically from time to time, to check the progress of your work.

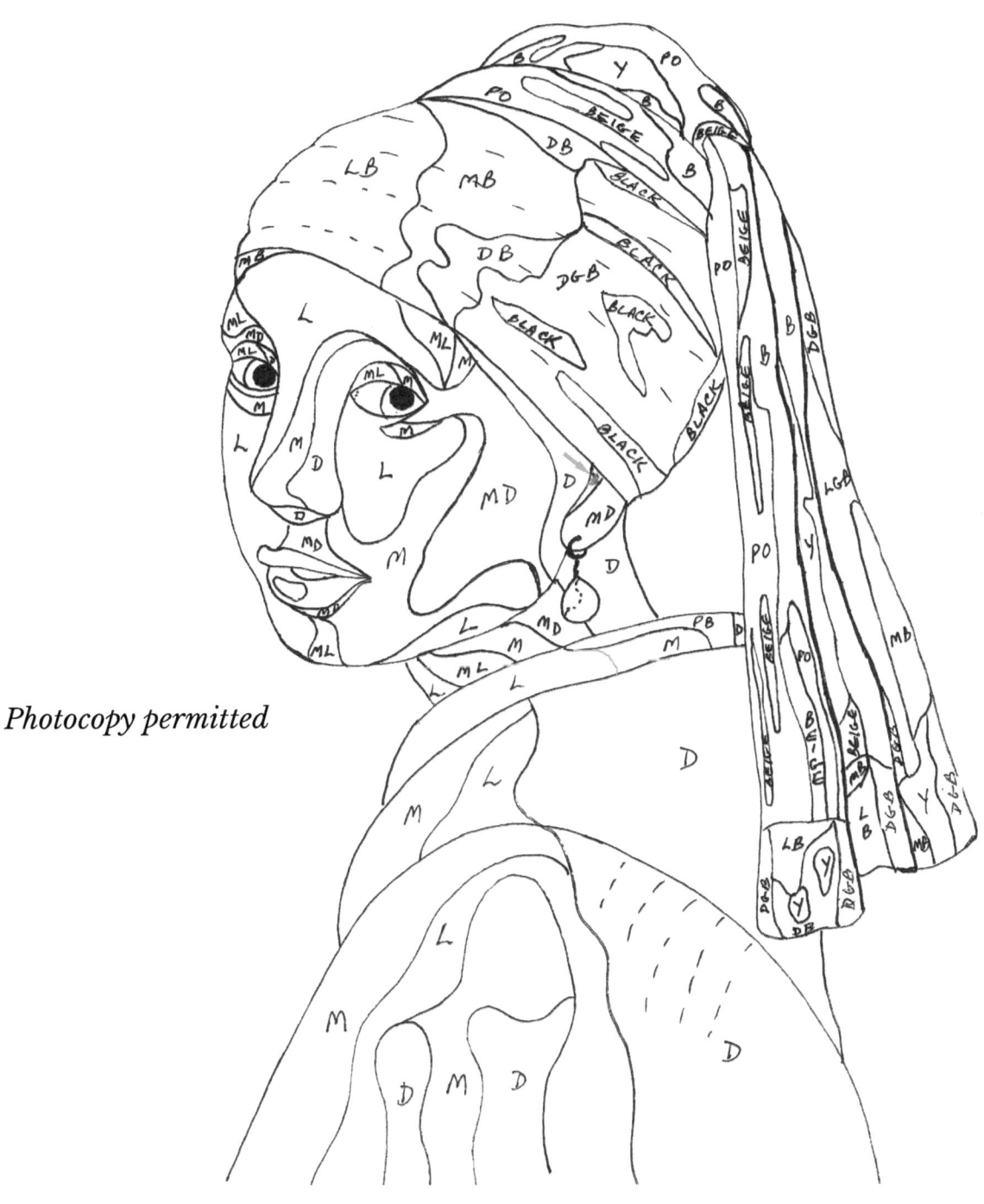

Photocopy permitted

Enlarging and Printing your Pattern

To get started you will need to enlarge your pattern by 235%.

You can scan the pattern into your computer and use the instructions below for resizing and printing your photo at home.

If you don't have a scanner, there is an app you can use to scan a photo or pattern, and it is available free through the Google Play Store or the Apple Store online, called PhotoScan by Google Photos.

Once you have scanned the photo, you can find it on your phone, email the picture to yourself, open it on your computer and proceed from there. Or perhaps you have a friend with a scanner who can help you out.

If none of these options works for you, then you will need to take the pattern to a copy centre and get them to enlarge and print the photo for you.

Enlarging can be done in a variety of paint or photo programs:

GIMP (free software – similar to Adobe Photoshop), Paint.net (also free), Paint (already on your computer- see below) and Photoshop Elements (can be downloaded as a free trial version).

Enlarging and Printing your Photo at Home

Check out my blog posts on how to enlarge and print your photo at home:

a) For the PC: https://valeriewilsonartist.com/step-by-step-instructions-for-enlarging-a-photo-and-printing-it-on-your-own-printer/

b) For the MAC: https://valeriewilsonartist.com/enlarging-and-printing-a-photo-at-home-the-mac-version/

Online options: (MAC or PC)

Rapid Resizer – Basic Version (this is a subscription program, currently about $15 CAN. for 3 months, so very affordable). This program allows you to resize any photo or pattern to whatever size you want and print it on your own printer.

You can also choose one part of an image (e.g. head) to enlarge to a particular size, and the rest of the picture will be sized proportionately.

The enlarged picture is printed out on numbered 8 ½" x 11" pieces of paper. Trim the borders, allowing some overlap for the adjacent page(s), and tape them together in order.

Other options: Photography shops, and Staples or other office supply stores, can also assist with enlarging and printing. You can copy your photo to a DVD or flash drive to take it to a printer/office supply/copy centre.

Some places such as Walgreen's photo (in the U.S.) will enlarge photos and return them to you via email, so check with your local stores about the services they provide.

Creating your Road Map

Now that you have the pattern enlarged, you are ready for the next step - transferring the pattern to a plastic overlay. This will help you to position the fabric pieces in the right places.

Tape your enlarged pattern to the foam core with the painter's tape.

Then place your plastic over top and tape it down so it won't move.

Using the Fine tip Sharpie, trace the pattern onto the plastic.

If you make a mistake or want to change a line, dip a cotton tip swab in the rubbing alcohol and use the swab to erase the line.

Pro Tip: Pour a bit of rubbing alcohol into a tiny container ready for use. Replace the cap on the rubbing alcohol right away so it doesn't get spilled or evaporate.

Pro Tip: Squeeze out excess rubbing alcohol before using the swab (just pinch it between your fingers).

After erasing a line, wait for a minute to let the rubbing alcohol dry or blot the area with a paper towel before redrawing your line.

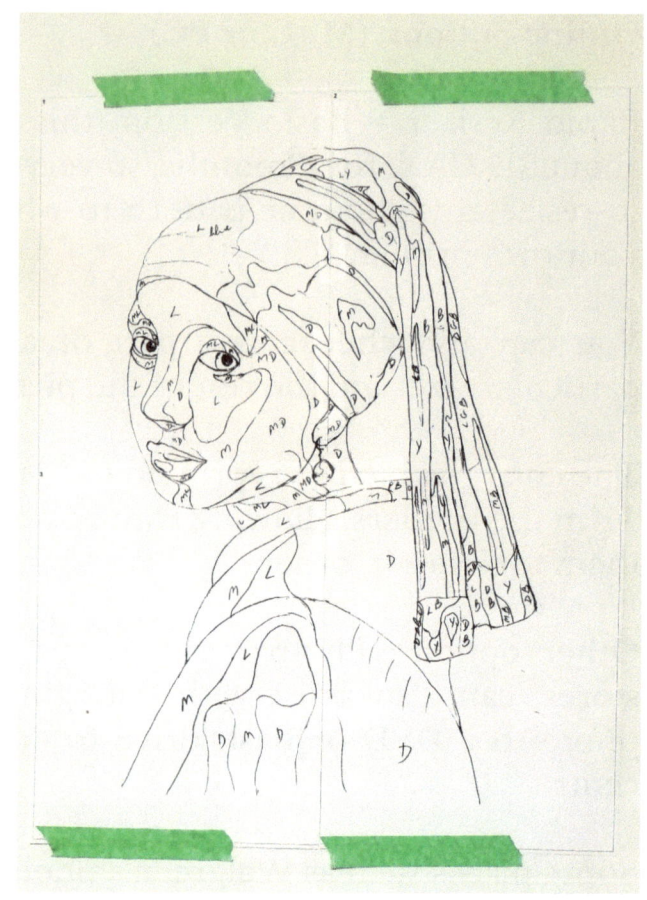

The Next Step

Now that you have your pattern ready to use, go to Chapter 2 for a look at values in fabric. Value (shadows/highlights) is the change from white through to black and all the grays in between.

You will need to have at least a basic understanding of value to be able to choose fabrics (Chapter 4) and start working on your portrait (Chapter 5). The change in value, from one piece of fabric to the next, is what gives your portrait dimension.

Pro tip: Don't skip this next chapter unless you are already very comfortable with distinguishing values!

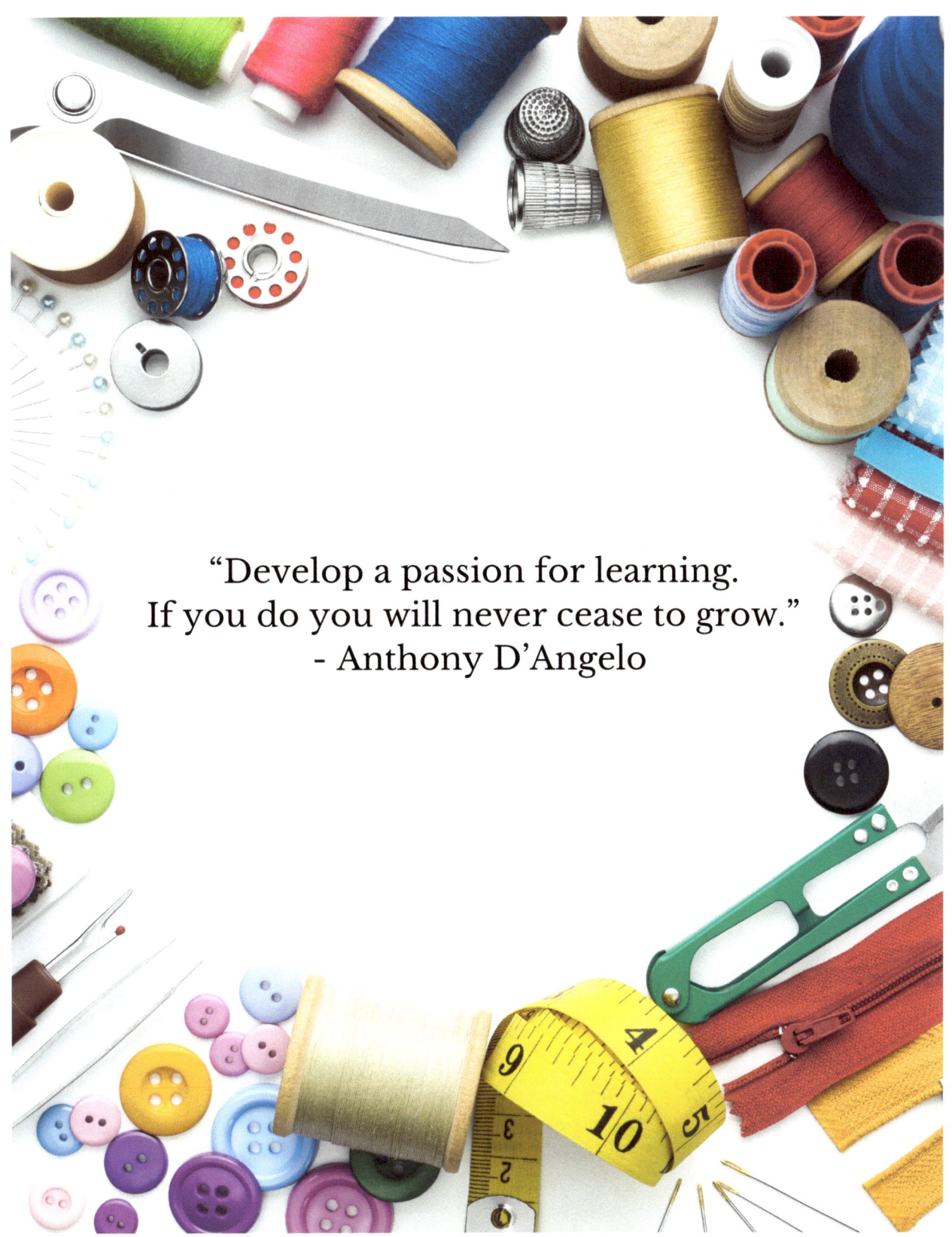

"Develop a passion for learning.
If you do you will never cease to grow."
- Anthony D'Angelo

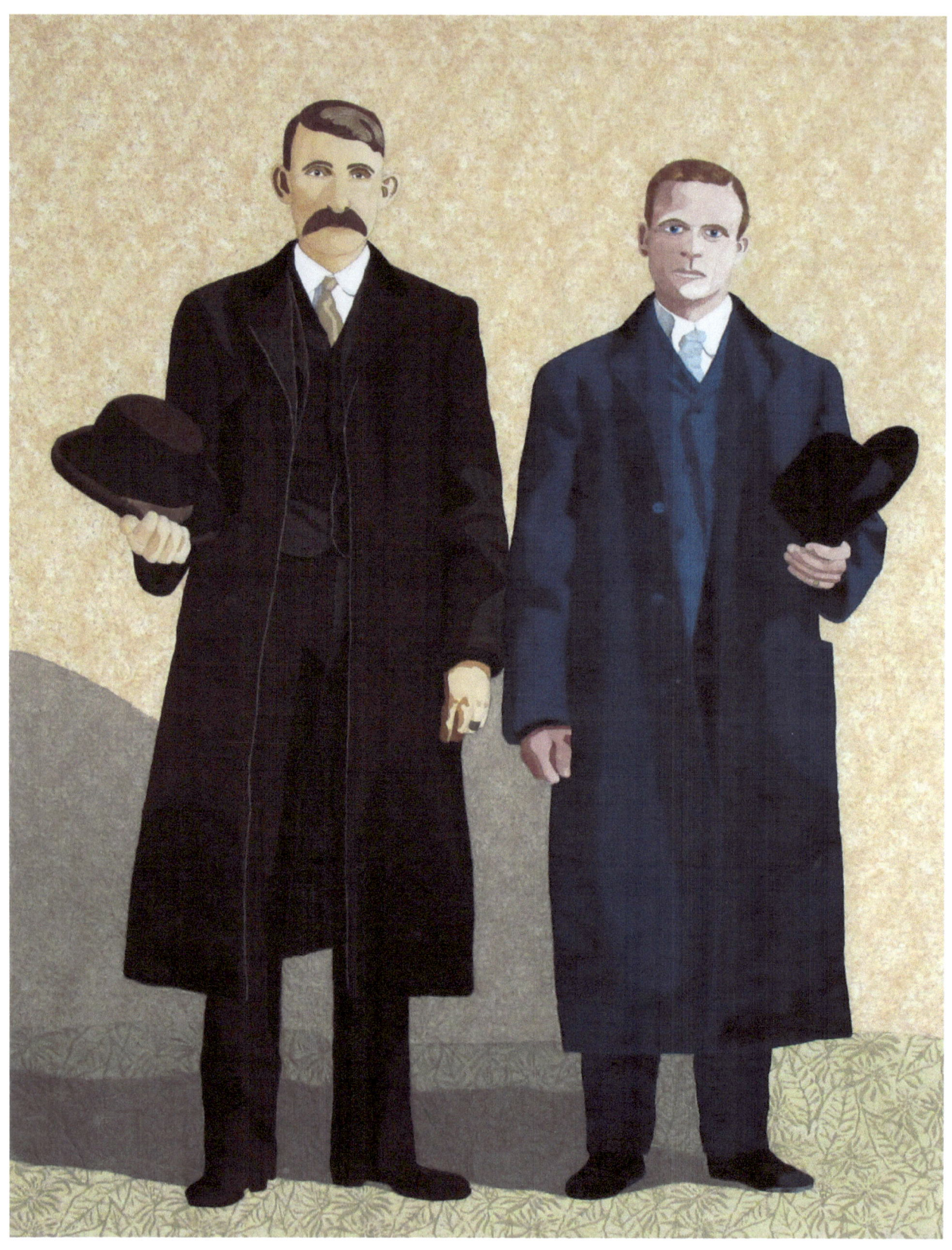

Chapter 2
Understanding Values

Why do we like one quilt more than another? Colour is certainly a factor. Bright colours attract the eye and make you stop and look. Soft pastels can create a warm, comfortable feeling.

Sometimes you look at a quilt and decide you like it, but it seems to lack something. It needs a bit of a spark to set off the design and give it some dimension.

One major factor is value, or how the lights and darks are distributed throughout the design. Careful use of value can make a design go from good to spectacular. Value is more important in a design than colour.

This is especially true when creating portraits in fabric. Correct use of value creates a realistic, three-dimensional look to a face.

Learning about value is one of the first critical steps in creating a fabric portrait.

What is value?

Value is the difference between black and white and all the grays in between.

Value is different from colour and it is important to be able to distinguish value separately from colour. Colour can distort your view of value.

Creating a Range of Values

For a quilt or a painting to sing, there needs to be a range of values.

I first learned about shading and highlights (value) and how effective it could be, in a folk-art painting class. It was somewhat magical!

The first step was to paint with a mid-tone colour, which unfortunately gave a very flat look. But this created the basis for the shape (in that case an apple).

To create form we added shading and highlighting. Suddenly the apple became rounded.

The challenge was to get the shadows dark enough and to have them gradually diminish in strength. The same process was used for the highlights.

Both the shadows and the highlights working together created the look of an apple you could pick up and eat. A range of values is what creates a three-dimensional look.

Contrast

If you want a dramatic contrast, put an intensely dark value next to a very light value. This makes for a very striking quilt but is not great for skin!

Gradation of Values

In a portrait what you want is gradual shading from one value to the next, so the whole face looks realistic and three dimensional, and avoids a patchy look.

How is this gradual shading achieved? It is through the careful selection of the values of the fabrics. A gray scale is an invaluable tool in this process.

Introducing the Gray Scale

It is important to understand what a value scale or gray scale is, and how it works. A gray scale has 6 - 10 values on it, ranging from black at one end to white at the other, and a variety of grays in between.

Artists use this tool to check the values in a drawing or painting. Quilters and art quilters use it for the same purpose.

Although, you can buy a gray scale at an art supply store, the best way to understand one is to make one.

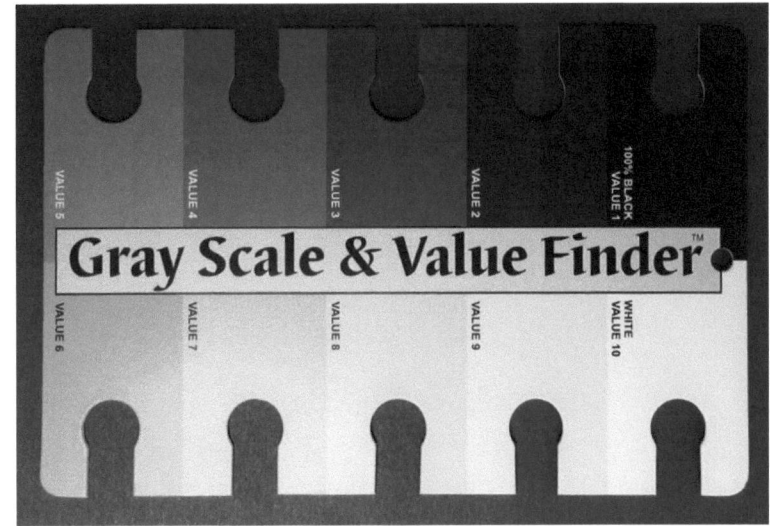

Creating a Gray Scale

For your first step, get a pencil and a piece of white paper.
1. Using a ruler, draw two parallel lines about an inch apart.
2. Draw vertical lines, an inch apart, to create 6 boxes.
3. Label the box at one end with White and the box at the other end Black.

4. Leave the box labelled White untouched, letting the white of the paper represent that piece of the gray scale.
5. Shade in the other boxes with the pencil, starting with the Black. You want this box to be as dark as you can get it.
6. Then fill in the other four boxes with grays. Each one should be slightly lighter than the previous one.

Pro Tip: Use the side of the pencil for shading. Apply more pressure on the pencil lead to get the Black value and less pressure as you move towards the White value. Also, you can shade up and down and then across to get a more even coverage. There should a gradual shift from one value to the next.

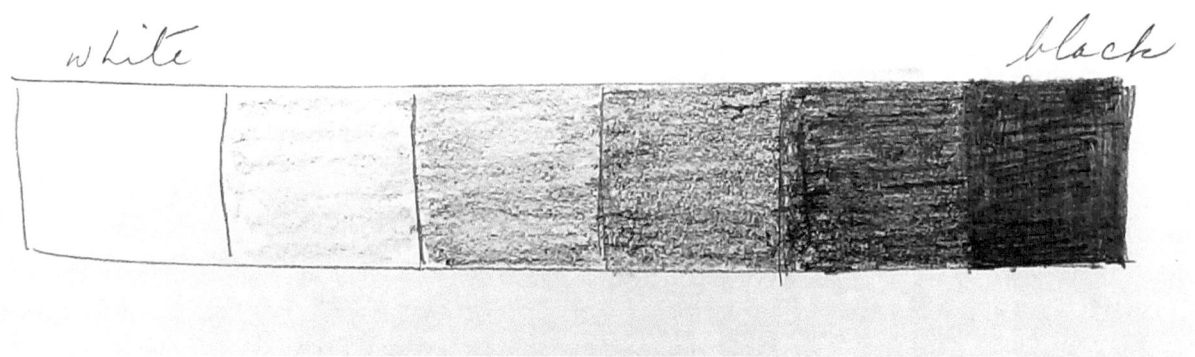

Check out this example of value and form. In this drawing, you can see how the shading creates form and depth in the composition.

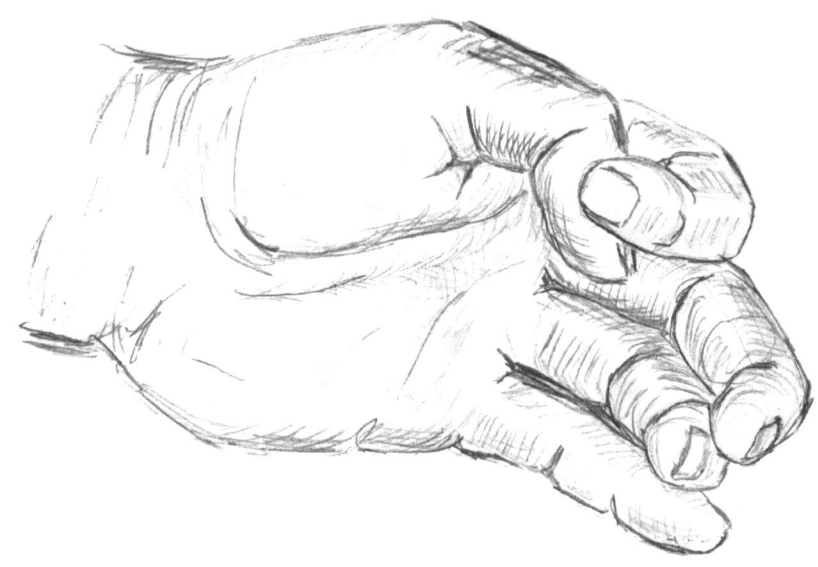

Later in this chapter we will be discussing how to achieve this effect with fabric. First, however, let's talk about relativity of value.

Relativity of Value

The value of a fabric is relative to the value of the one next to it. Sounds strange, doesn't it?

Here is an example: All the centre fabrics are the same colour (hue) and value. Note how different they look next to different values of fabric.

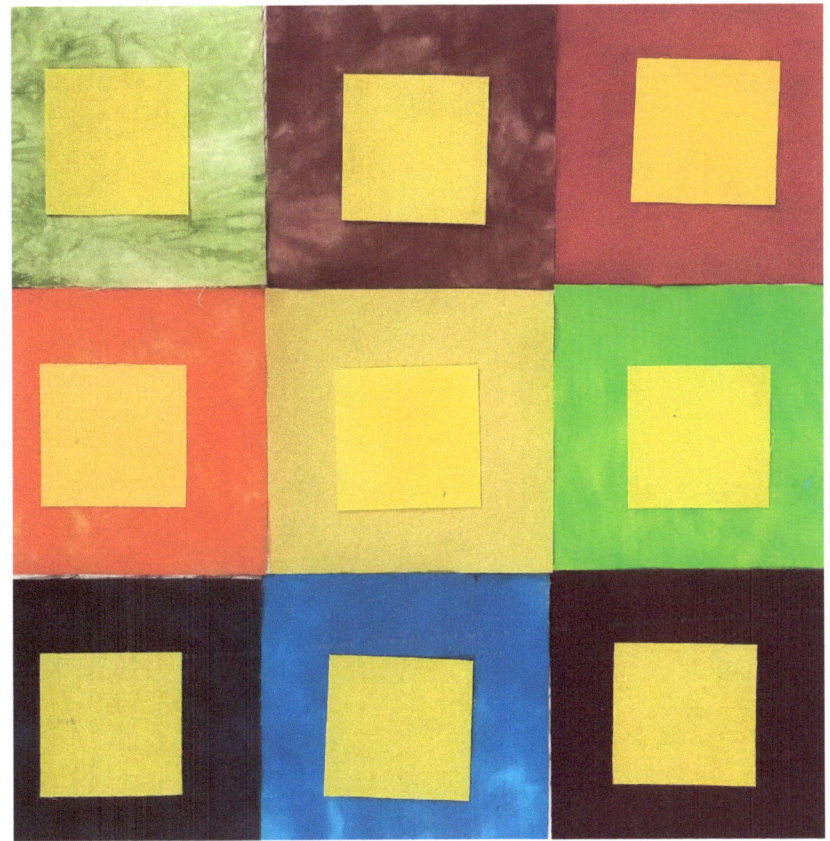

Relativity of value is **important to understand** for a couple of reasons:

• So that you can **select the appropriate range of values** in fabric for your portrait and thus get the **right shading**, which creates dimension in a face.

• So that your **portrait** will **stand out from your background**. If the face is pale, then a darker background will enhance your portrait because of the difference in value (contrast).

If the value of the face and the value of the background are too similar, the face will tend to blend into the background.

Creating a Gray Scale in Fabric

This is what a gray scale might look like in fabric. There are four values, from a light value on the left to a dark value on the right.

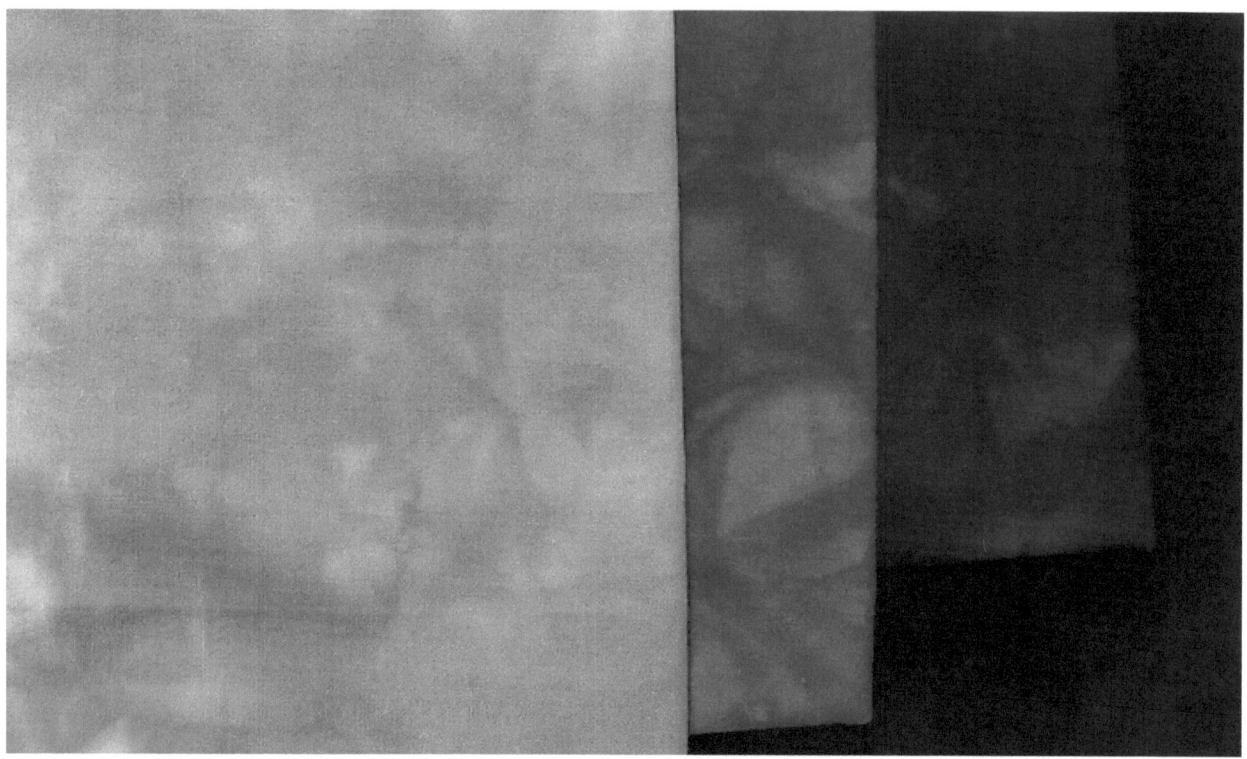

An Exercise using the Gray Scale

1. Take the gray scale you created and either punch holes in each value or cut out a small section at the edge of each value. It can help to glue your gray scale to cardboard to give it some stiffness, making it easier to handle.

If you would prefer to use a commercial gray scale, you can order one here: artisticquilts.net

A commercial **gray scale** allows you to **place the card over your fabrics** and look through the holes to **determine the value**.

1. Go to your stash and select some gray and/or black fabrics, preferably solid colours or tone on tone. Dark blue fabrics will work too. If necessary, call a friend, and use her stash and have some fun.

2. Sort the selected fabrics by value. To select a gradation of values, place the gray scale over each of your fabrics and try to match the value on the scale, as closely as possible to the fabric.

3. Try and find 4 - 5 values of fabric that form a smooth gradation.

Value in Coloured Fabrics

Once you get comfortable with value in black and white, it is much easier to determine the value of coloured fabrics.

Here are some photos that may help:

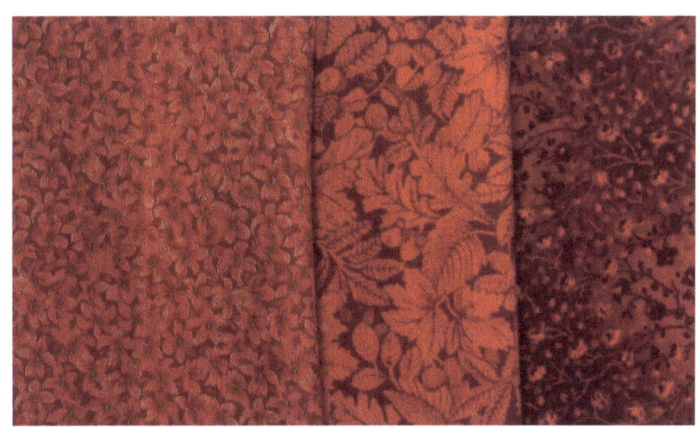

Example 1

This first set is reds which are subtly patterned fabrics. They look pretty good as a value gradation, but are they? Let's check!

Ways to check the values of your fabrics

It is much easier to see the values of your fabrics by viewing them in black and white. Here are 3 ways to do that:

1. With your camera or your phone, take a picture of the fabrics you have selected and change the photo to black and white.

   • On some cell phones, you can go into colours and change the photo to black and white right on your phone.
   • When I look at a photo on my android phone, I can change a photo to black and white under effects (the icon looks like 3 interlocking circles).

2. Use your cell phone and an app called PhotoScan to scan your fabrics. Works for Android (find it in the Google Play Store) or iOS (find it in the Apple App Store).

3. Scan your fabrics on a scanner. using the black and white option.

   • If the lid sits too high when you have the fabric on the scanner bed, simply drape a dark piece of fabric over the lid of the scanner to block out excess light and then do the scan.

Once you have a picture of your fabrics in black and white, review it to check the values. For a portrait, you want a smooth gradation, while for another quilt you may want contrasting values.

When we look at those red fabrics in black and white, they do look good as a value gradation.

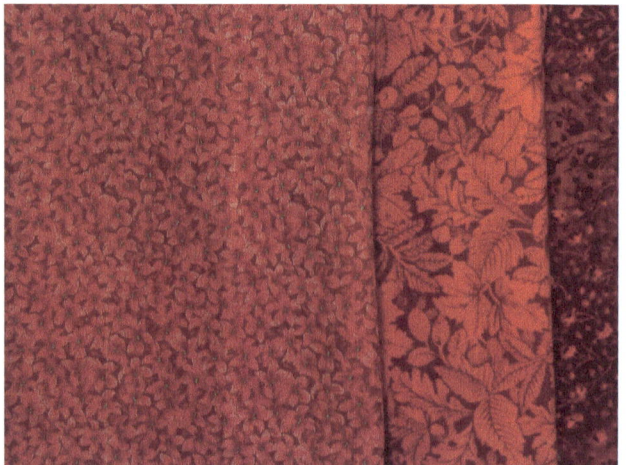 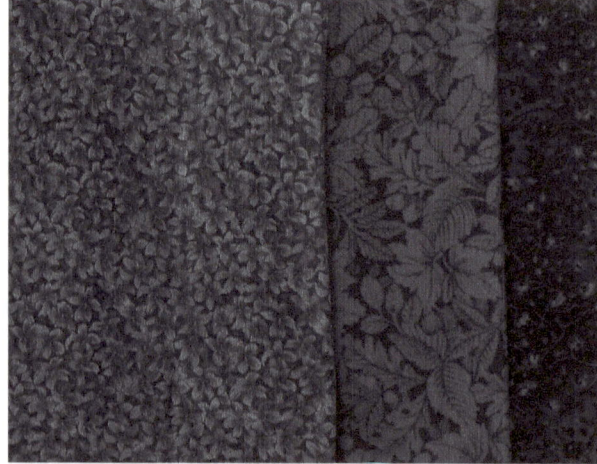

Example 2

These teal fabrics are another example. The first photo shows them in colour and the second one in black and white.

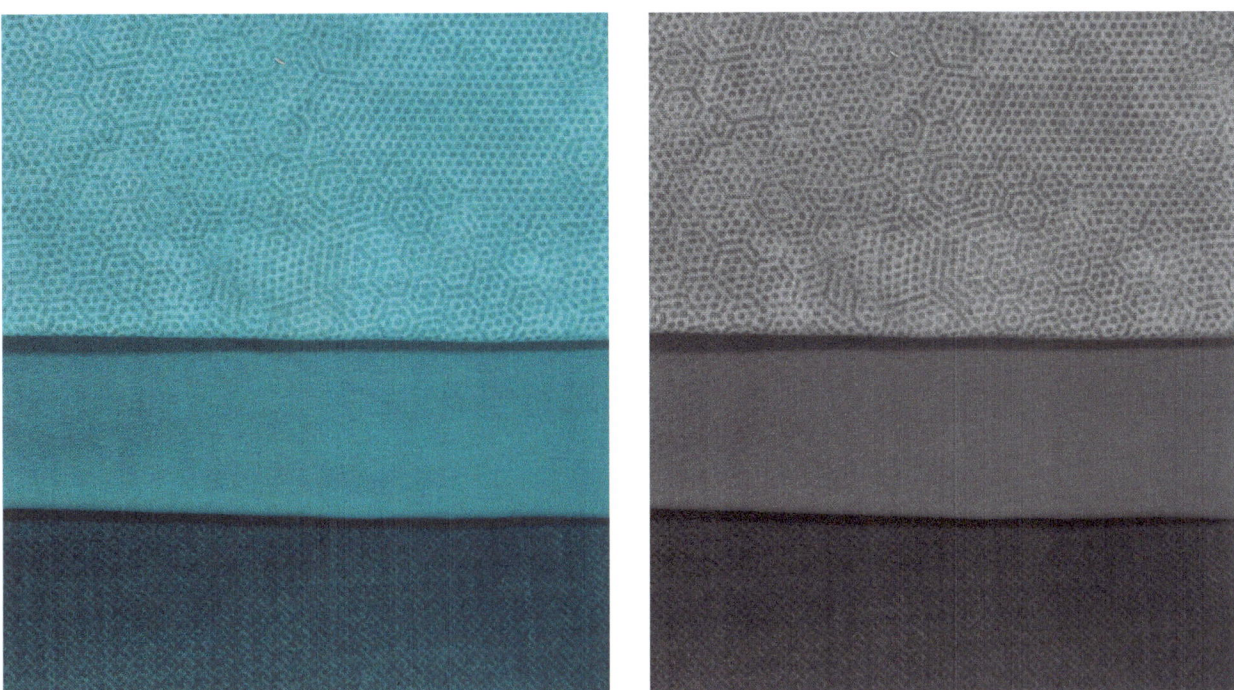

Here, there is a jump in value from the lightest value to the second value. Another fabric could be added in for a smoother gradation depending on what look you are trying to achieve.

The fabrics shown previously were used for clothing (reds) and a car (teals) in one of my portraits. The following photo shows that art quilt.

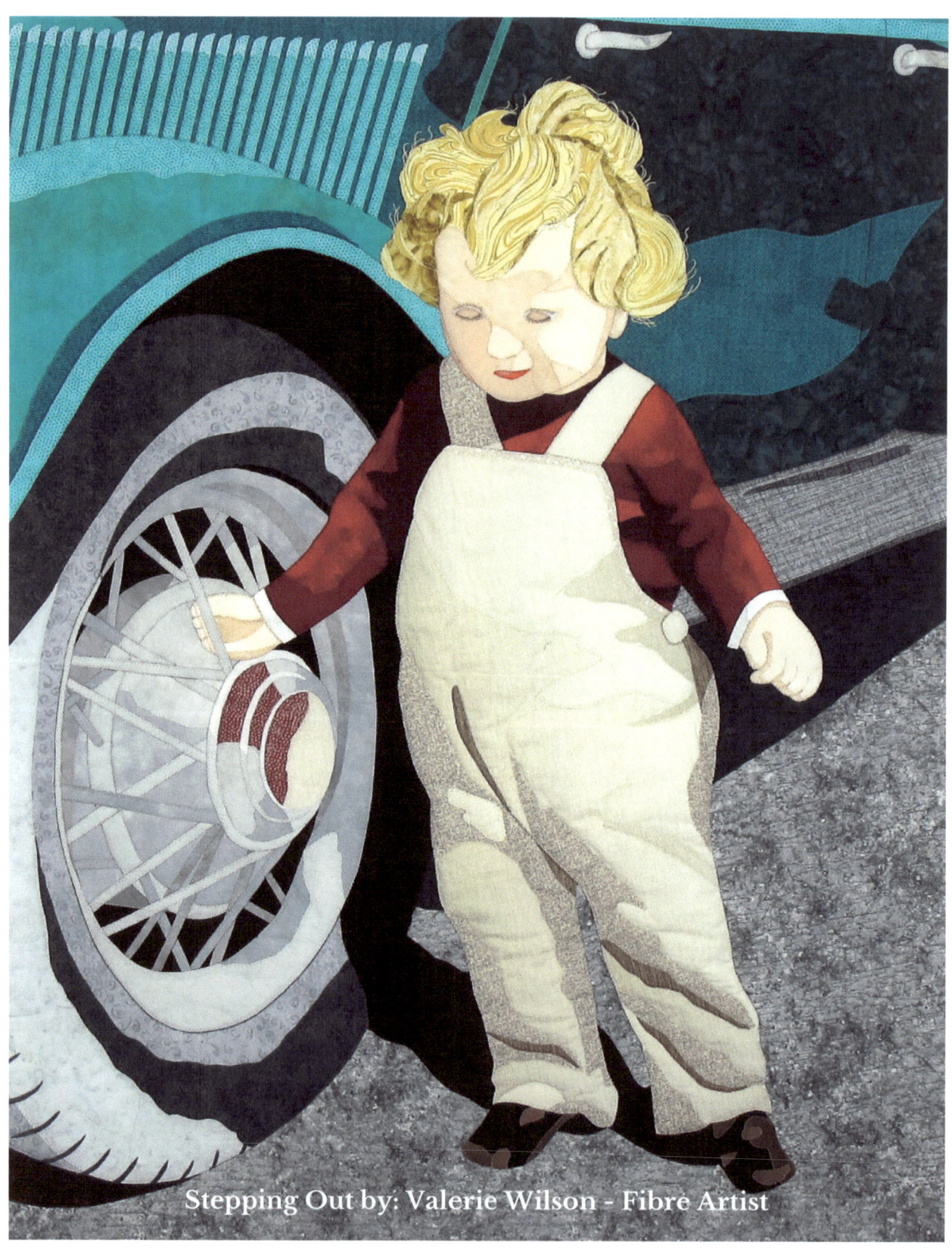

Stepping Out by: Valerie Wilson - Fibre Artist

Using Printed Fabric

Prints in fabrics can deceive the eye because of the different values in the print. It helps a lot to convert them to black and white to double-check the values.

If you would like to use prints to create a portrait, be sure to choose ones that do not have too distinct a pattern, as these types of fabrics can be hard to blend. The best options are fabrics with subtle or small prints.

Also, for a portrait, try to avoid those fabrics which have white or very pale colours in the design on a dark background. The sharp contrast in values distorts our perception of the overall value. Save those fabrics for other uses.

Skin Tone Fabrics

As I mentioned before, in a portrait, the effect you want to create for the face and other skin areas is a subtle gradation of values.

You want each fabric to be a slightly different value than the next, so the person's face does not look patchy.

I used 5 values of fabric for the skin tones, in the portrait of the child with the car (shown previously).

Colour Choices

I use my hand-dyed fabrics for skin tones. If you would prefer, you can purchase a set of skin tone fabrics for this portrait we are doing together.

My store is: artisticquilts.net

Here is one example of a 5-value set of lighter skin tone fabrics. These are the colours that I used in the portrait of the Girl with the Pearl Earring.

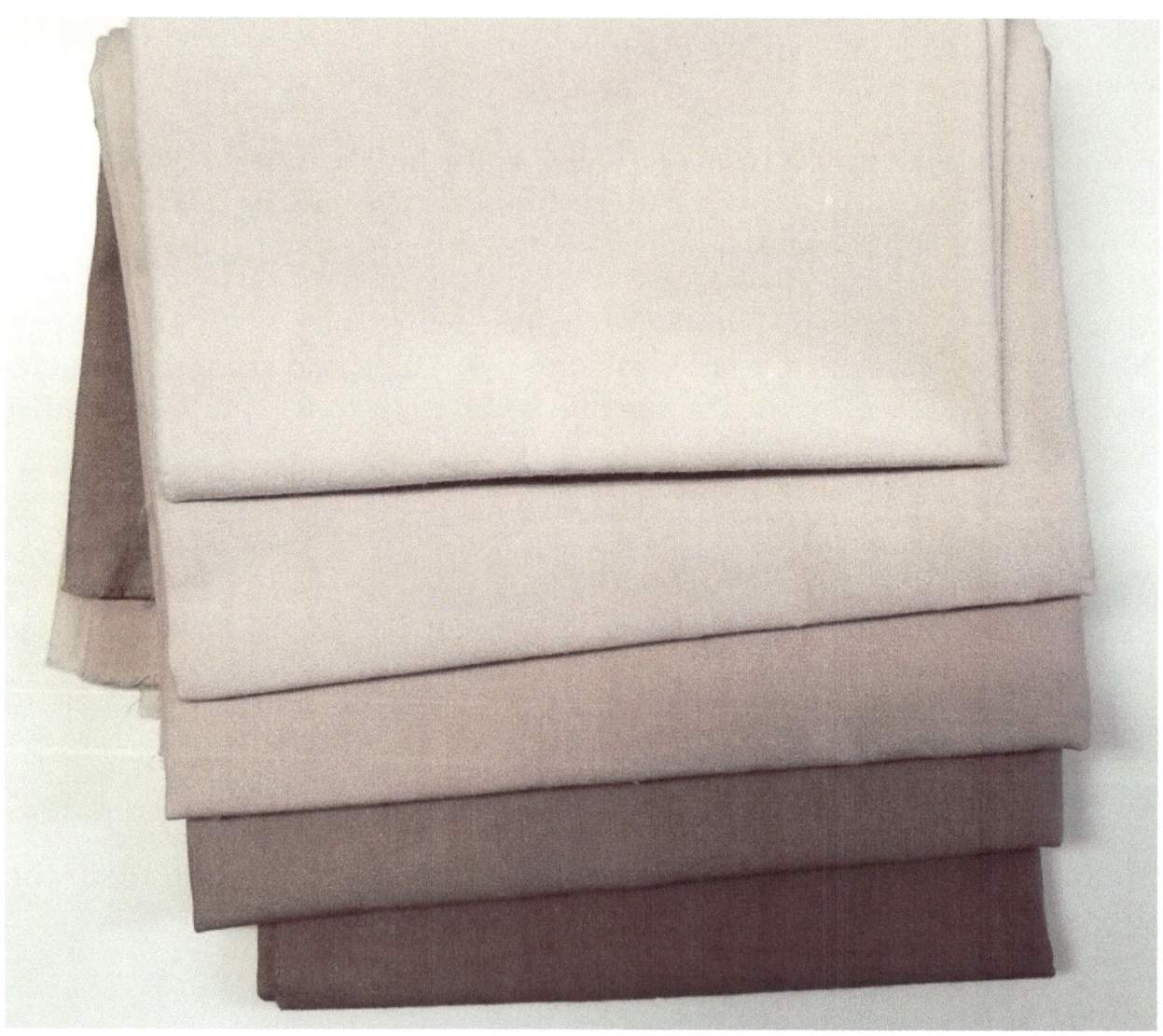

If you are interested in seeing the infinite variety of skin tones in the population, check out the Humanae project (link in the Resources section of the book). The researcher matched numerous people's skin colours to Pantone colour chips. This could give you some ideas for the skin tone fabrics you might want to use.

Now that you have an understanding of values, we will go on to fabric selection in the next chapter.

"Your reality is a reflection of your strongest beliefs"
– Steemit.com

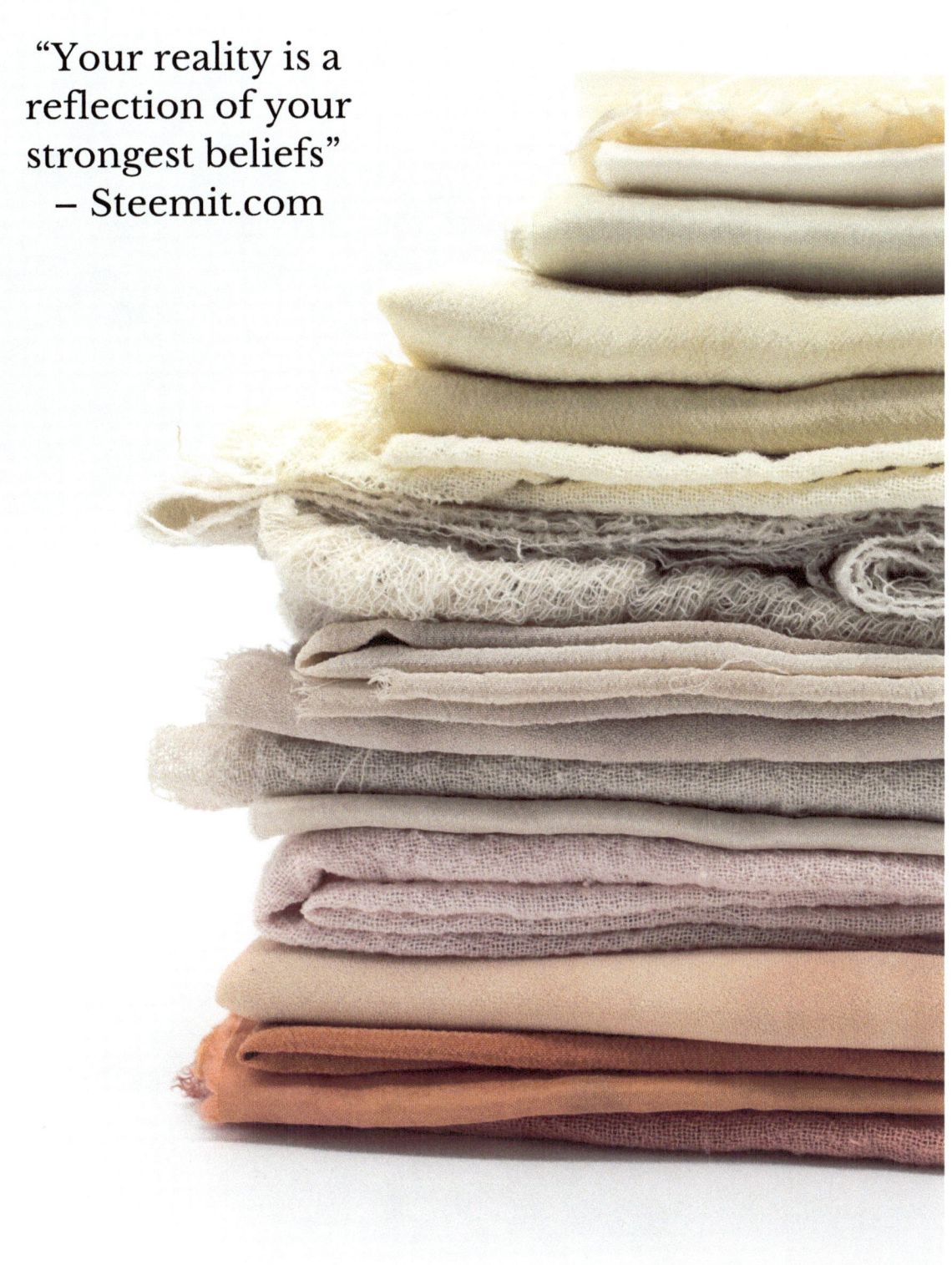

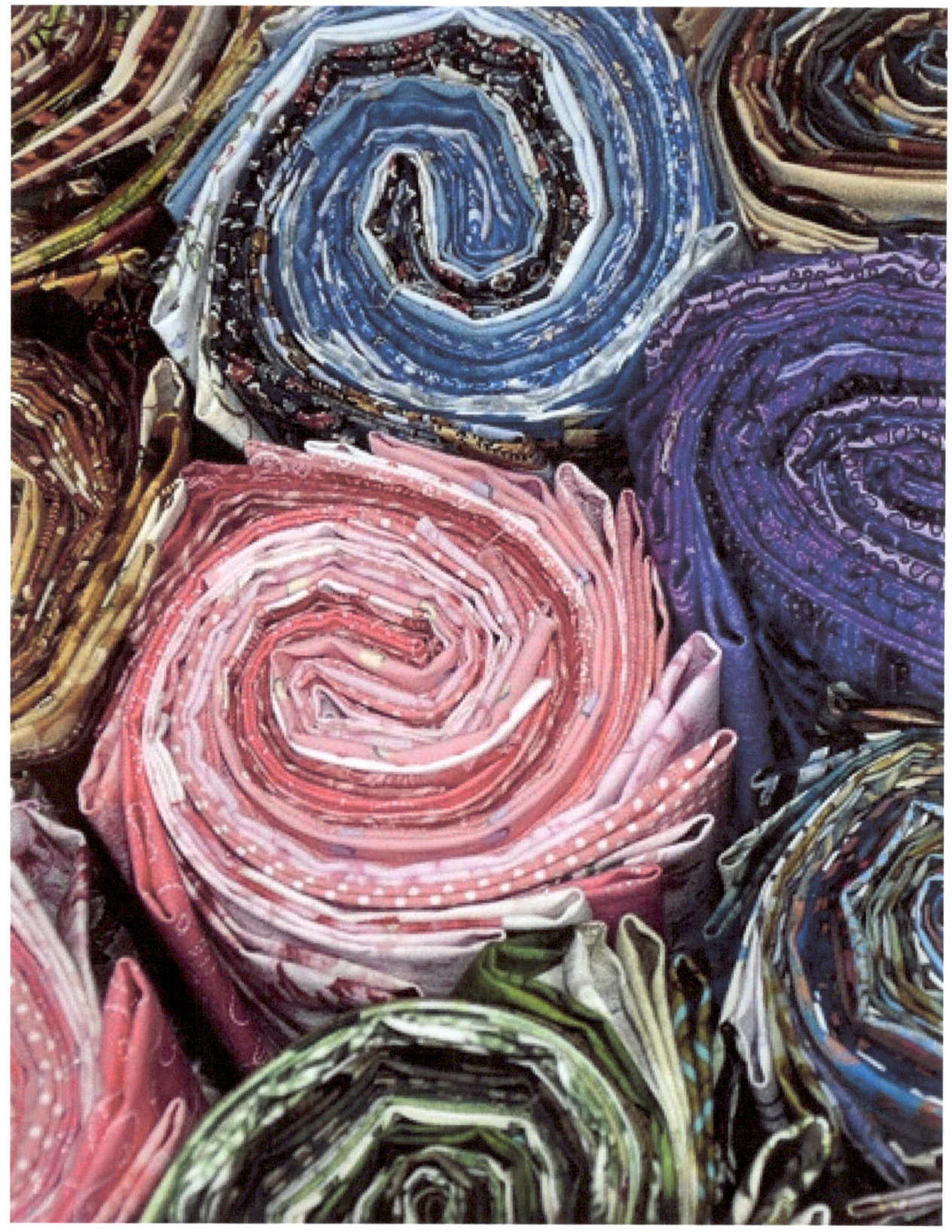

Chapter 3
Choosing Your Fabrics

Prewashing

It's a good idea to prewash your fabric so the Lite Steam-A-Seam® 2 (recommended fusible) will stick more easily. Don't wash really small pieces of fabric in the washing machine as the edges will fray. You can hand wash them and hang them to dry. Also, when cutting your fabric allow some extra for shrinkage when washing and drying it.

If you want to use similar colours to the ones I used for the original version of The Girls with a Pearl Earring, then follow the list below. Depending on your fabric stash, you may be able to use scraps for some of the pieces.

Fabrics for my version of the Girl with a Pearl Earring

Refer back to this photo and the photo of the finished piece, as an aid in choosing your fabrics.

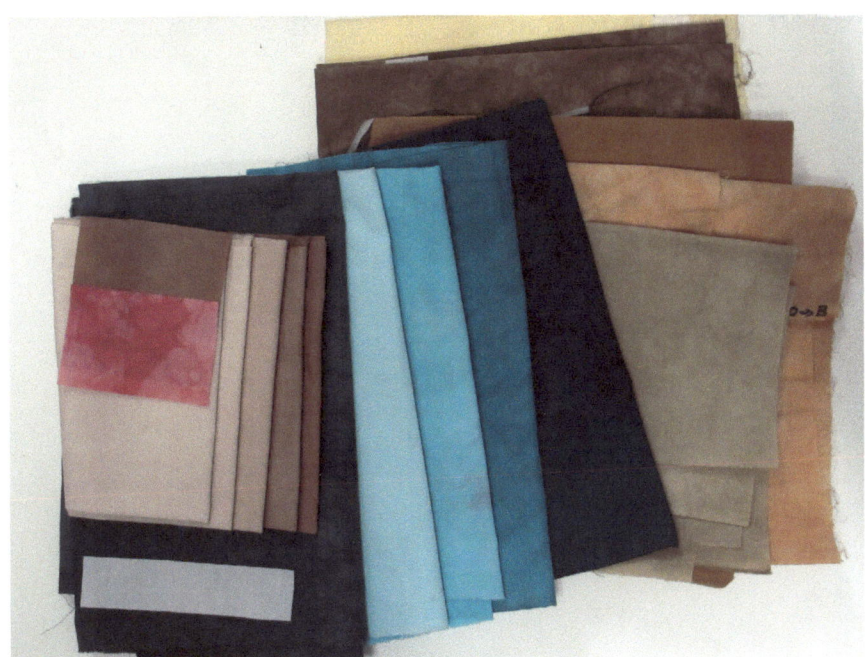

Pro tip: Fabric is often sold in quilt shops as "fat quarters" which are one half of a half yard or 18" x 22". Quilting fabrics are generally 44" wide. Fat quarters are very convenient for a project, like this one, that takes small quantities of several different colours of fabric.

Fat eighth – 9" x 22"
Fat sixteenth – 9" x 11"

When the size of a piece of fabric is indicated, that means you will need that minimum amount of fabric, to easily cut out the shapes for the project.

Skin tones

- 6 values – 5 of the light to dark values, each in a fat 1/16th and one - piece of a very dark value approximately 3" x 3" in size.

Gown

- Light Orange - Fat eighth
- Medium orange - Fat eighth
- Medium brown - gown and scarf - Fat eighth

Collar and earring

- Very pale blue approximately 6" x 1" (for the collar)
- White - approximately 7" x 3"

Head scarf

- Pale Orange - Fat eighth
- Medium Beige - approximately 6 " square
- Very pale yellow - approximately 9" x 3"

Blues - I used a slightly turquoise set of blues for most of the fabrics:

- Light Blue: approximately 6" square
- Medium Blue: Approximately 6" square
- Medium Dark Blue: Approximately 6" square
- Dark Grey Blue: Approximately 8" square
- Medium Grey Blue: Used for her eyes and the tail of the head scarf - small strip approximately 7" x 3"
- Black – approximately 6" x 4"

Lip colour

- Medium red – approx. 3" x 3"

Background

- Black (or colour of your choice) – at least 22" x 27"

Backing fabric

Choose a colour and/or pattern of fabric of your choice for the back of your quilt. The quilt backing is the fabric that goes on the bottom of a quilt sandwich. It consists of the quilt top (right side up) as the top layer, then batting below that and then the backing fabric (right side down). The backing fabric is placed so that the right side is showing on the back of the quilt when you flip it over. You can use regular quilting cotton or other similar fabric.

Allow extra fabric for creating a sleeve for hanging the quilt which will be placed at the top of the back of the quilt. I usually allow for a piece of fabric that is the width of the quilt (as above) by 9" to have enough fabric to create a 4" sleeve. So, in this case the fabric for the sleeve would need to be 22" x 9".

Instructions on creating the sleeve will be discussed in Chapter 8.

Choosing your own colours for your portrait

If you want to choose your own colours, keep in mind the values needed. You may also decide to simplify the tail of the scarf. This is easy to do as some small pieces are laid on top for accent/highlight.

For a more interesting composition think in terms of complimentary colours (opposites on the colour wheel). In the original I used blue and orange with white and black as neutral colours. The oranges and blues were all toned down colours (gray added to subdue the colour) rather than bright clear colours.

It is a good idea to have a colour wheel to help you when selecting colours.

Primary Colours

Red, Yellow, and blue

Secondary Colours

These are the colours that are created by blending two of the primary colours which are side by side. For example, yellow-orange is a blend of yellow and orange. You can see the secondary colours on this colour wheel.

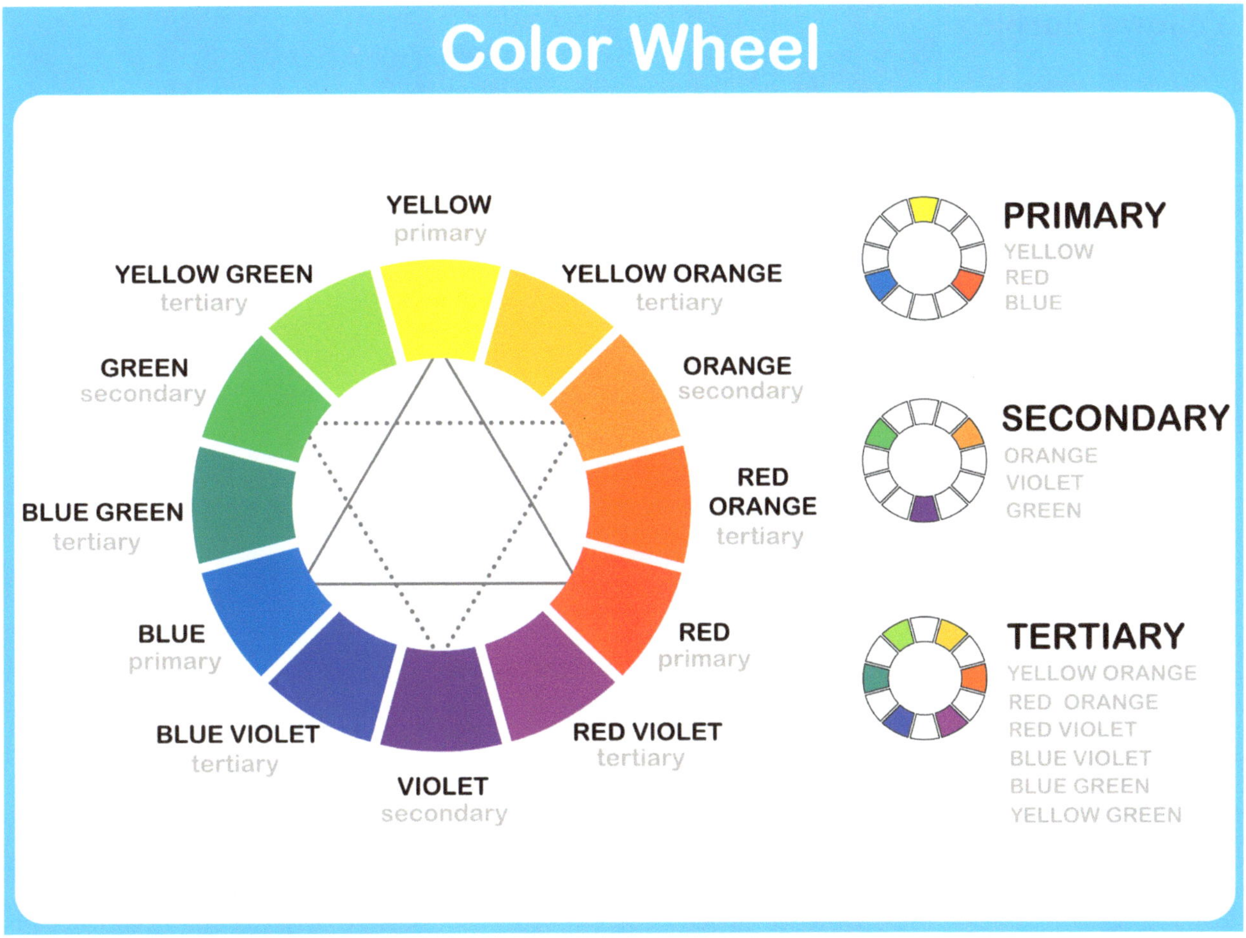

Color Wheel

PRIMARY
YELLOW
RED
BLUE

SECONDARY
ORANGE
VIOLET
GREEN

TERTIARY
YELLOW ORANGE
RED ORANGE
RED VIOLET
BLUE VIOLET
BLUE GREEN
YELLOW GREEN

Complementary Colours

These colours are opposite each other on the colour wheel and can add interest to a quilt. It is best to let one of the colours be dominant as equal amounts of each colour can be harsh. Consider using the complements of the secondary colours as well.

Some examples of complementary colours (using the primary colours) are:

Red - Green

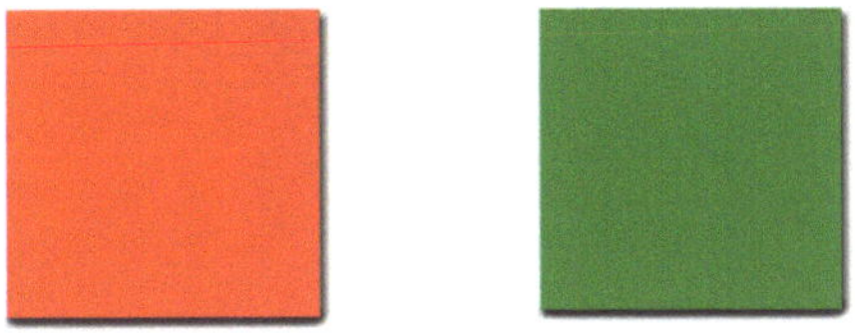

Yellow - Purple

Blue - Orange

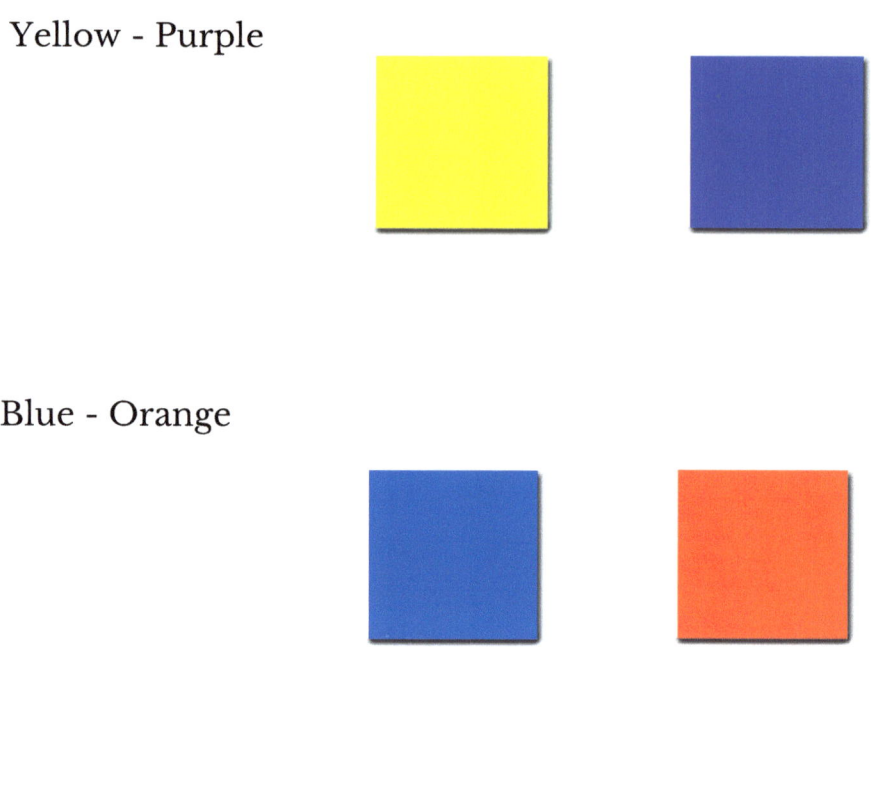

Using Lite Steam-A-Seam 2 ®

I like to use the Lite Steam A Seam 2 ® for my fusible as it is sticky on both sides. Thus, it will stay in place when working on a design wall or when moving the project around. It is also great because it allows fabric pieces to be easily moved around or replaced as needed.

Apply fusible to each whole piece of fabric before you start cutting. You will be cutting a variety of shapes out of each value of fabric.

Note: There isn't any need to put fusible on the background or backing fabrics.

When using the Lite Steam-A-Seam 2 ®, remove one side of the paper backing (whichever side comes off easily) and using your hands, press the fusible to the back of the fabric.

If the fusible does not seem to be sticking well, try rubbing firmly with your fingertips. You can also try a warm iron (NO steam), running the iron quickly over the front of the fabric. You may need to repeat this process a couple of times.

Pro tip: Too much heat or holding the iron still for too long can cause the Lite Steam-A-Seam 2 ® to fuse permanently to your fabric and the backing paper!

For more tips on using Lite Steam-A-Seam 2 ®, check out the blog post on my website called: "Lite Steam-A-Seam 2 ® Top 10 Tips for Success" you can find it at https://valeriewilsonartist.com/steam-a-seam-ii-lite-top-10-tips-for-success/

You do not want to fuse down the pieces of fabric until you are happy with the final result. This means that it is easy to change out pieces of fabric, if needed.

Other fusibles

If you can't find Lite Steam-A-Seam 2 ®, there are a wide variety of other fusibles that you can use. Check with your local fabric store to see what they recommend. I would suggest picking one that is lightweight so that it doesn't add too much stiffness to the project. Follow the instructions for the fusible that you choose.

If you are using a fusible, other than Lite Steam-A-Seam 2 ®, you will need to use pins to hold all the pieces in place until you get to the fusing stage. I would suggest appliqué pins which are shorter than the usual straight pins. You can simply poke these into the foam core to hold the pieces in position.

On to Chapter 4 to start creating your portrait!

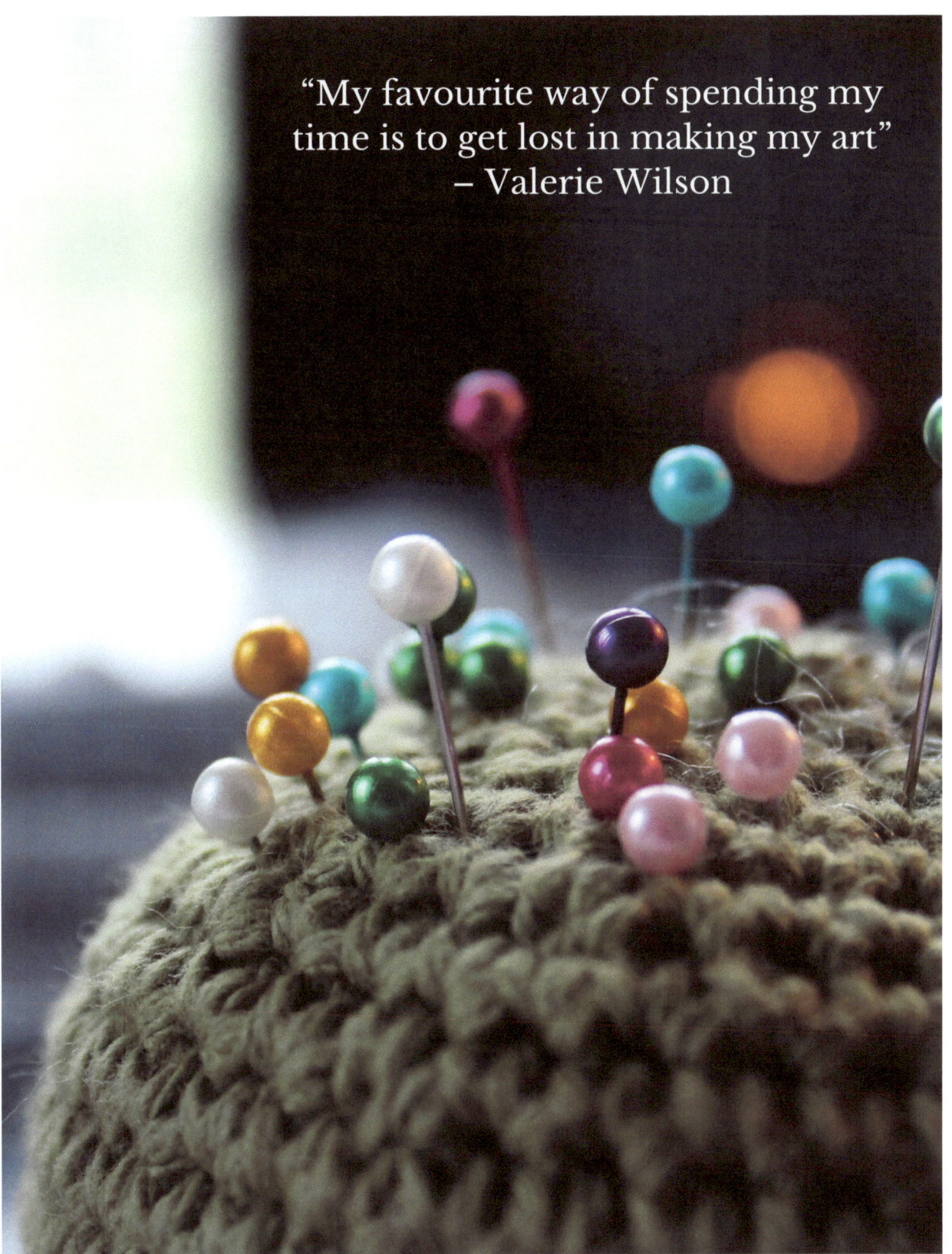

"My favourite way of spending my time is to get lost in making my art"
– Valerie Wilson

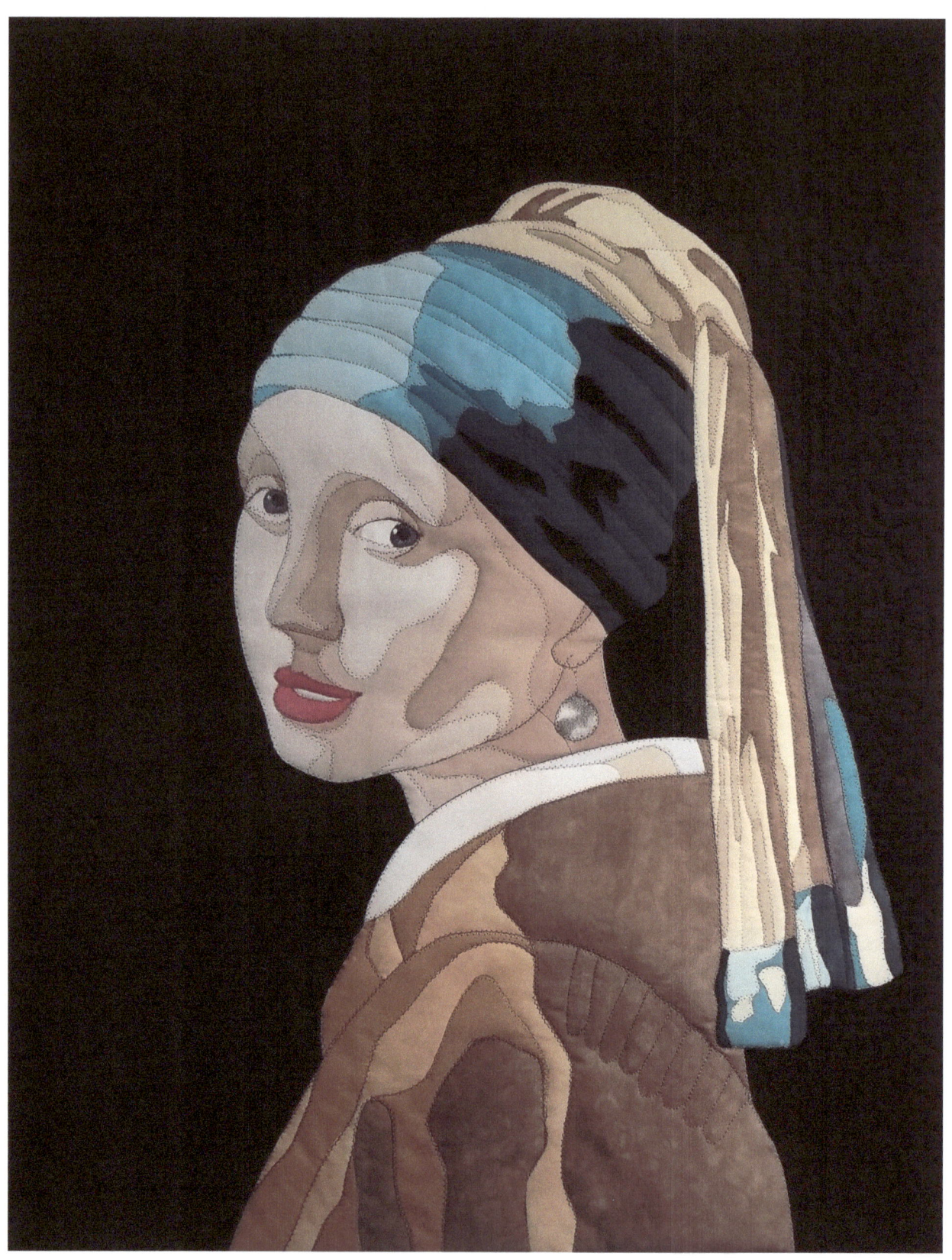

Chapter 4
Creating Your Portrait

Before you can get started creating your portrait, there are a few things you need to do to prepare.

Preparation

a. Remove the pattern and plastic overlay from the design wall (foam core)
b. Now using the painters' tape, attach the white foundation fabric to the foam core. Do not pull the fabric too tight, as you don't want to stretch it.
c. Using the painter's tape, attach the plastic with your pattern on it, over the foundation fabric. Secure the plastic at the top only, as you want to be able to easily lift the plastic and position your fabric pieces underneath.

Pro Tip: Using a Sharpie or other pen put an X in the two lower outside corners of your foundation fabric. Trace these same X's onto your plastic (pattern) overlay. You will use these registration marks to line up the pattern as you work and make sure that the pattern is not shifting around. If the pattern moves out of place as you work, you will end up with a distorted face.

Starting the Portrait

1. Take your original picture, and pin it up alongside the design wall or have it close by so it is easy to see for reference.

2. You will use 6 values for the skin tones in this portrait. It is a good idea to mark each of your fabrics (in a corner) with the values they represent. You will thank yourself later!

3. Remember to mark the values/colours for the clothing fabrics as well.

In the picture of the fabrics I used for this project, there is also a piece of dark pink, hand-dyed fabric that I used for the lips.

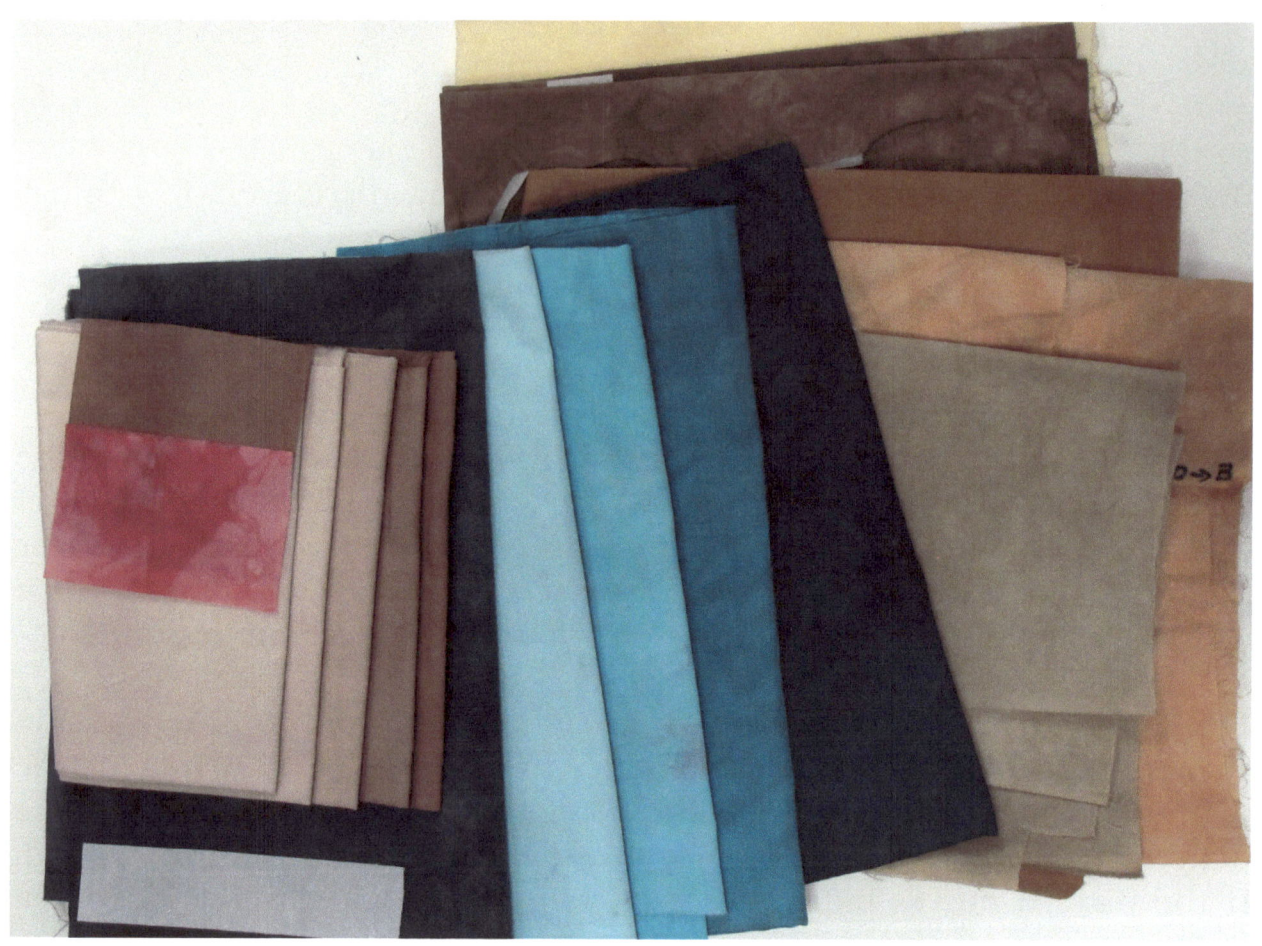

Tracing the Pattern Pieces

Each of the shapes you will need for the portrait is traced one at a time from the pattern and placed immediately afterwards onto the base fabric. This prevents any confusion as to which piece is which.

More importantly, this will help you to know what lines are pattern lines (hard) and which edges need to be extended to go under another piece of fabric, that will be added later.

In this method of applique, the tracing is NOT reversed.

Pro Tip: check which edge or edges of the shapes need to be cut on the line. For example, the outside edges of the face, neck, and gown, need to end on the lines.

Also, once you have placed your first piece of fabric, the next piece will be cut on the pattern line (hard line) on one edge and the other edges will be extended slightly to go under the next piece or pieces. Remember, if the piece ends at an outside line (e.g. edge of face), then the piece is cut on the line at that edge as well.

When you go to trace the shapes from the pattern, keep in mind which edges are to be on the line of the pattern and which ones need to be extended. You can either trace these lines further out or add little arrows to indicate a larger size on that edge.

On any edge that will later be overlapped by another piece of fabric you will need a little extra (about 1/16") so will cut them slightly larger. Try to keep this extra fabric to a minimum, as the darker fabrics will shadow through the lighter ones (even more so once you fuse them!).

To start, place a piece of tracing paper over the first segment (usually the darkest value) on the pattern. Trace the shape with your pencil as indicated previously.

Don't worry if occasionally you forget! It happens to all of us. Just trace and cut another piece and continue.

Fabric Placement

Apply fusible to the back of each of the pieces of fabric before you start (no ironing needed). You can put the fusible on only a small part of the fabric if so desired.

In the case of the face, however, I would recommend applying the fusible to the whole piece of fabric. This will save you some work, as you will be cutting a variety of shapes out of each value of fabric.

Instead of pins, use binding clips to hold your tracing paper in place on the top of the fabric. Pins used with Steam a Seam 2 Lite ® will leave dark glue marks on lighter fabrics and gum up your pins!

When placing the fabrics, you start with the section of the portrait that is farthest away or is underneath another section. In this case, you will start with the neck as it is the farthest back in the portrait.

The long-handled tweezers are invaluable at this point for slipping the pieces into place as you don't need to lift the plastic very high to get underneath. This makes positioning your fabric pieces easier.

The order of fabric placement:

1. Neck
2. Eyes
3. Rest of the Face
4. Ear
5. Head scarf (only the part in the blues on her head)
6. Gown
7. Remainder of the scarf in sections

Values for the Skin areas

Follow this list of values for the skin fabrics you will use for the neck, face and ear. The placement of these values is marked on the pattern.

D = Darkest value
MD = Medium Dark
M = Medium
ML = Medium Light
L = Lightest value

Pro Tip: Remember to mark the values on your fabrics to avoid confusion. It is easy to pick up the wrong value and then find out, only when you place the piece, that it is the wrong value. Having done this many times, I now mark my fabric. It makes for less stress.

Placing the Fabrics (please read this whole section before starting)

The dashed lines on the headdress and the shoulder of the gown are a reference for quilting and can be ignored at this point.

In each section, start with the darkest value of fabric. Place those pieces first. Then work on the next darkest value and so on, until you have completed that section.

Be sure to check your placement when adding fabric pieces to the foundation fabric. Check that your pattern has not shifted! If it has shifted, reposition it and the fabric pieces underneath it or you will get a distorted image.

Pro Tip: The pearl will be added on in a later step on top of the neck fabrics, so ignore it for now.

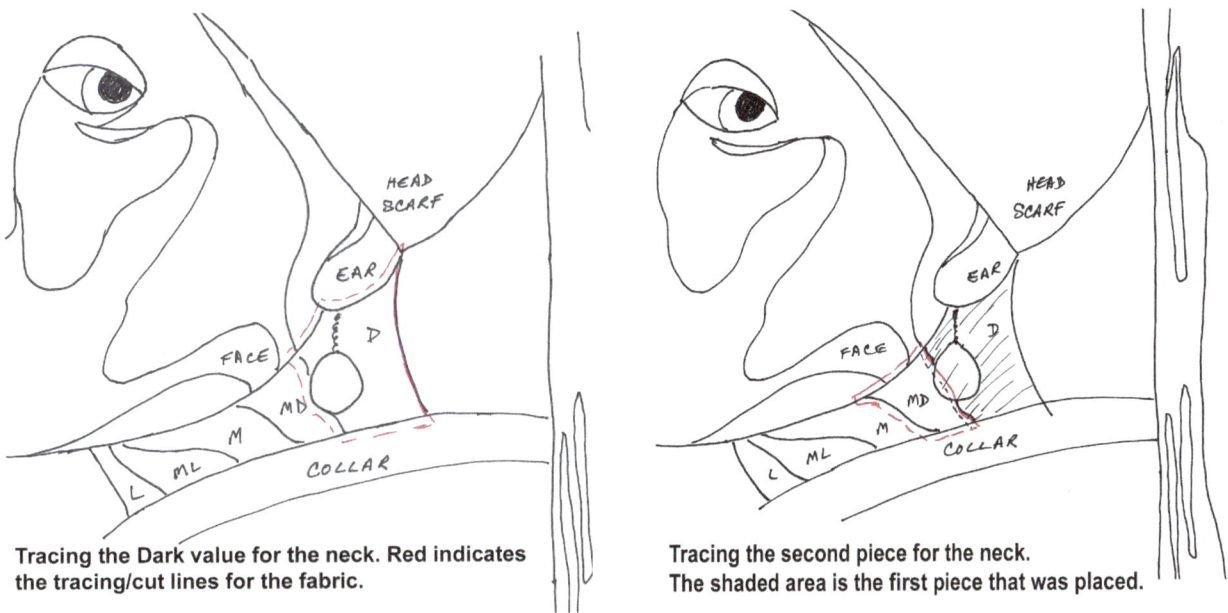

Tracing the Dark value for the neck. Red indicates the tracing/cut lines for the fabric.

Tracing the second piece for the neck. The shaded area is the first piece that was placed.

1. Using a small piece of tracing paper, start by tracing the piece for the darkest value on the neck (as seen on the previous page). Use this as a pattern to be placed on the right side of the fabric you are using.

2. Continue with the next value (medium-dark) and so on until you have placed all the values of fabric for the neck.

Once the neck is completed, you will start work on the eye area. The eyes are completed before the face, as the eyes sit back in the head.

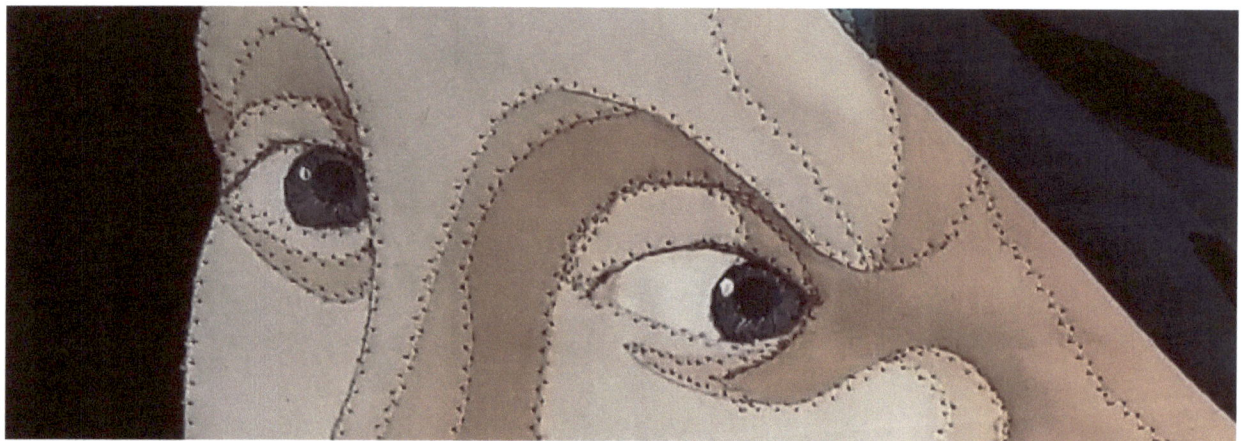

Eyes

Note: The circle template is used for tracing the shape of the iris and for adding the pupil to the eye.

1. For the eyeball (white of the eye), you will use a piece of white or slightly off-white fabric.

a. Trace the eye shape from your line drawing on to a piece of tracing paper, adding 1/16 of an inch all around the piece, so that the piece of fabric is bigger than the eyeball. This is important as the white fabric will be covered on all the edges by the face fabrics.

b. Using your plastic overlay as a reference for placement, place the piece of fabric that you are using for the eyeball on the foundation fabric,

2. Iris. Next is the iris of the eye. Using the circle template, place it over your plastic overlay and determine what size circle you will need for the iris.

Pro tip: Note the iris is a circle but the edges are partly covered by the eyelids.

Using the circle template, trace the circle for the iris onto your eye colour fabric (grey-blue). Cut it out carefully, being sure to maintain the round shape. Place this piece in place on the white eye fabric.

Note that you will be adding detail to the iris later on.

3. Pupil. I use the circle template and a black Micron Pigma pen .08 to create the pupil.

Pro tip: Look carefully at your tracing to determine the size and placement of the pupils. The circle template works well for determining the size. Allow a little extra room for the edge of the template to get in the way.

Once you are sure of the position of the iris, put the appropriate size circle of the template in the correct place for the pupil. Holding the template firmly, use the Pigma pen to fill in the circle with ink.

Pro tip: Don't worry if you make a mistake, simply take off that iris fabric and cut out another one and try again.

4. Adding the highlight can be done at this point with white acrylic paint (as described below) or later detailed with thread (see Chapter 6).

Pro tip: Be sure to check your portrait for the direction of the lighting and the placement of the highlights in the eyes. Note that both highlights are at the same height and on the same sides of both eyes. (See the picture of the eyes)

If have decided to use paint, place a small drop of the paint on a piece of tracing paper or plastic lid. Use a pin or stylus to dip into the paint. Test the amount of paint on the tip by tapping it lightly onto a piece of coloured fabric. If this looks Okay, dip again and add the highlight to the iris.

6. Adding a tiny piece of pink or paler red fabric to the inside corner of the eye on the right makes it look more real, as well. The corner of the eye on the left is hidden behind the nose, so doesn't need this additional piece of fabric there.

Face (Please read this entire section before starting)

Have your 6 values of face fabric laid out from dark to light.

1. Referring to the line drawing, continue with the placement of fabrics for the face.

2. Start with the darkest values in the face for your fabric placement. Note the exception for the nose area below*.

Before cutting each piece of fabric, note on your tracing paper which edge or edges need to go under another piece and need to be extended, and which edges are to be cut on the line.

Pro tip: Place the light value fabric on the left side of the face and then put the sliver of the medium value fabric under the eye.

*Nose: I placed the dark fabric over the edge of the light cheek fabric. Then I added the medium and light value fabrics to complete the nose and forehead.

Pro tip: Place small scraps of the face fabrics on the outer edge of your foundation fabric as you work. These scrap pieces come in very handy later for trying out your thread colours and stitching later on.

Lips

Cut each of the lips out separately from the fabric. The bottom lip is placed first and then the top lip. The white of the foundation fabric shows inside the open mouth.

Note that the upper lip is darker than the lower lip, as it is in slight shadow. Also, note that the lower lip has a highlight close to the centre on the left.

Pro Tip: The lower lip can be fussy cut from a mottled fabric so that the highlight appears in the right place on the lip. An alternative is to use a white coloured pencil to add a subtle highlight. If you need the top lip darker you can shade it with a coloured pencil.

Ears

Add theses 2 pieces of fabric now, as they are on top of the face and neck in this portrait.

Clothing

The next step is the clothing. By using the careful placement of the various values of fabric you will create the look of folds and wrinkles in the gown and headscarf.

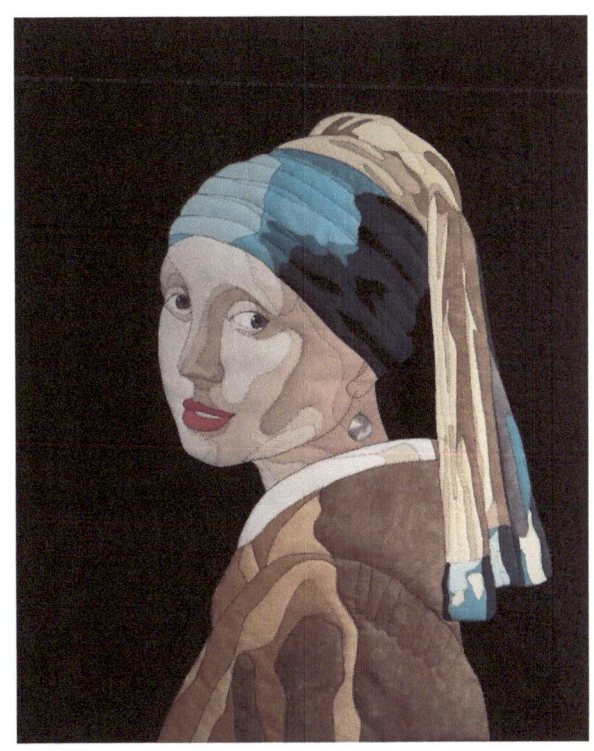

Collar

1. Start with the collar of the gown. For the darkest part (by the tail of the head scarf), I used a tiny piece of the medium brown colour, from the fabric for the gown. Next to that is the Pale Blue.

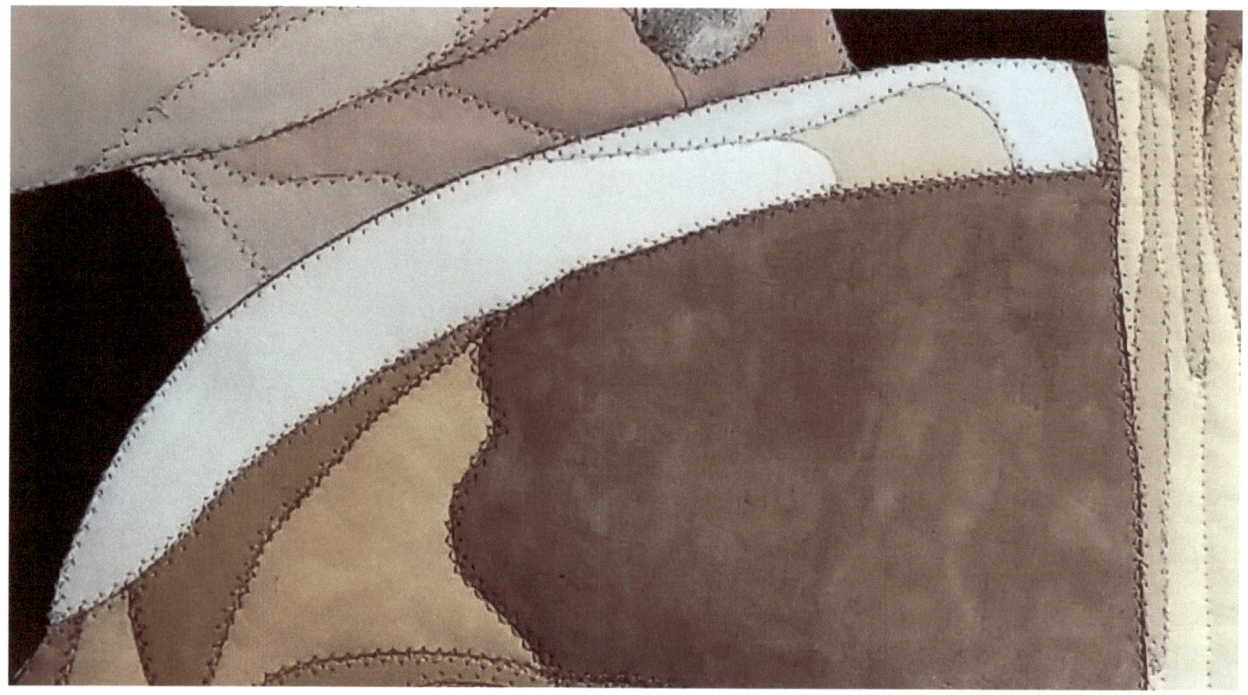

2. The medium value on the collar is the Pale Orange fabric that will be used later on for the medium value in the top part of the headscarf.

3. The light value is White.

The top part of the gown (high collar)

Place the dark, medium and light values of fabrics that are for the gown starting with the dark value first.

Dark – Medium Brown
Medium – Medium Orange
Light – Light Orange

Shoulder and the main part of the gown

Place the gown fabrics, as per the previous instructions for placing the values of fabric.

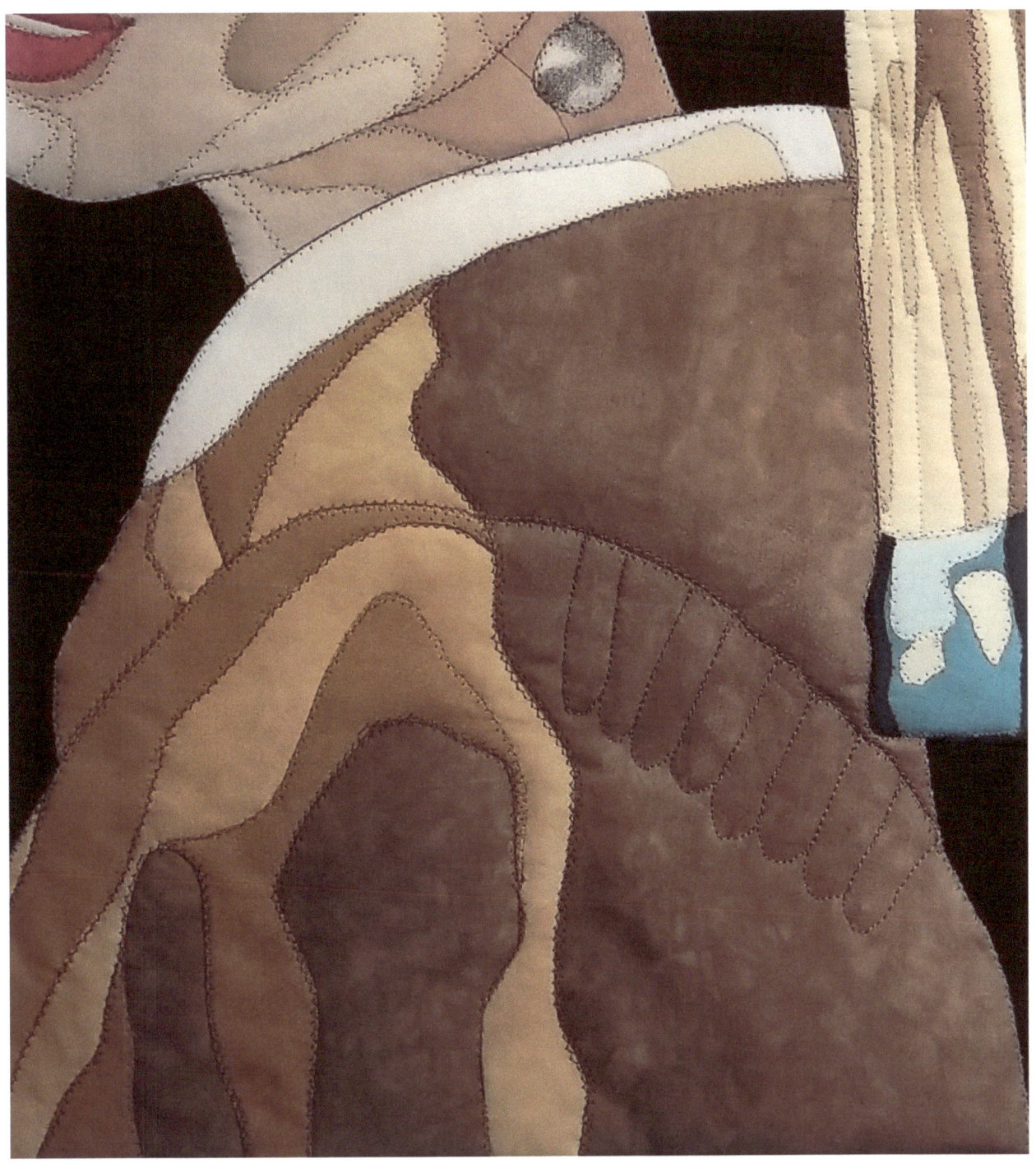

Head Scarf

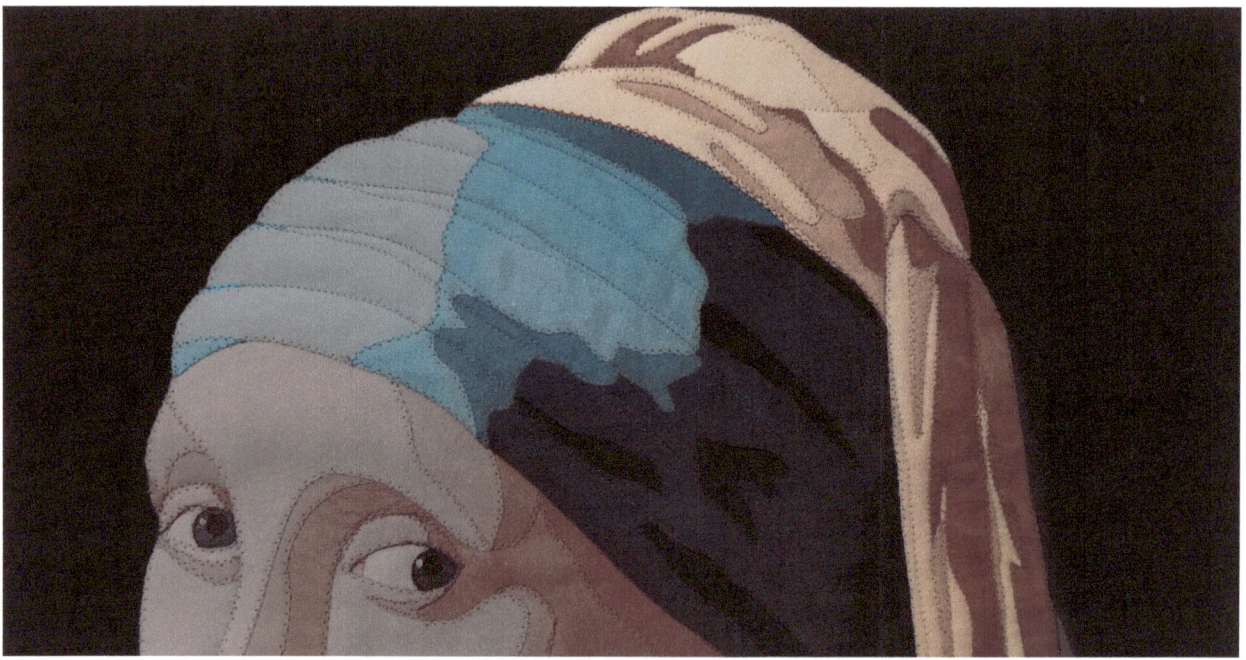

Topmost Part of the Scarf

This part of the scarf uses the Pale Orange, the Medium Brown of the gown and the Light Yellow.

Dark value - Medium Brown (B)
Medium value – Beige

Note:

The small piece of the medium value (Beige) is set to the side for the moment. It will be added later after the tail of the scarf is in place.

Medium Light value – Pale Orange (PO)
Light Value – Light Yellow (Y)
Start with the darkest value as usual.

Now you can move on to the next section down on the head scarf.

Middle Top Section (head scarf) – just above the blue

This section uses the Medium Brown, the Beige and the Pale Orange.

Dark value – Medium Brown (B)
Medium Value – Beige
Light Value – Pale Orange (PO)

Head wrap section of the scarf

This section uses the Blue fabrics and the Black fabric listed for the head scarf.

Dark Value – Dark Grey Blue (DGB)
Medium dark value – Dark blue (DB)
Medium value – Medium Blue (DB)
Light value – Light Blue (LB)
Accents/shadows - Black

Pro tip: I added the Black fabric on top of the other fabrics for the easiest placement.

1. Start with the darkest value - the Dark Grey Blue fabric.

2. Then the Dark Blue and so on.

3. When you have all the blue fabrics in place, cut out and add the Black pieces on top.

Pro Tip: As you did with the Black on the head wrap, place any fabric pieces that are "islands", i.e. completely surrounded by another colour/value, on top of the underlying fabric. This saves you from trying to cut around these little areas and simplifies fabric placement. This includes the Beige slivers of fabric, and the yellow on the bottom of the tail of the scarf closest to the girl.

Tail of the scarf (See the abbreviations on the pattern)

There are 3 sections to the tail of the scarf. Start with the part of the tail that is furthest right.

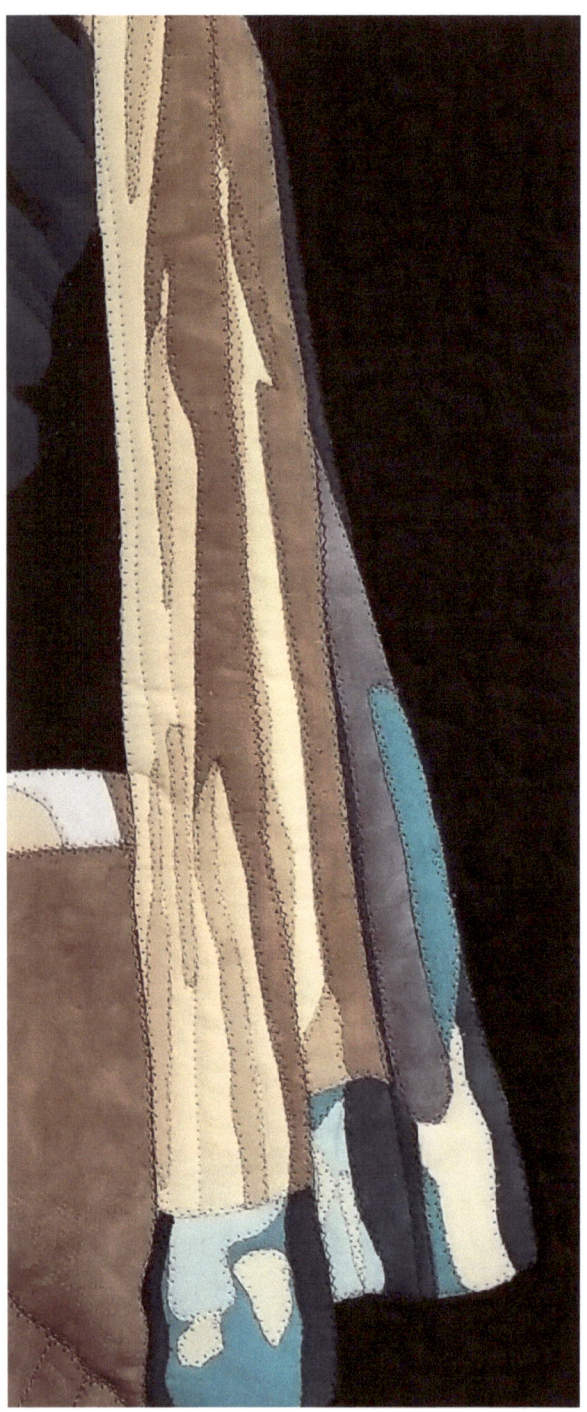

Start with the furthest section of the tail first.

Colours used in the tail of the scarf:

Dark Grey Blue (DGB)
Medium Blue (MB)
Light Blue (LB)
Light Grey Blue (LGB)

Medium Brown (B)
Beige
Light Orange (LO)
Pale Orange (PO)
Yellow (Y)

1. Once the first section is completed, work on the next section and so on.

2. Now that the tail of the scarf is complete, add that small piece of beige at the top of the tails (see the Note in the section on the Topmost Part of the Scarf).

The next step is to add the pearl.

You will need a small piece of white fabric (left over from the collar) with Lite Steam-A-Seam 2® on the back.

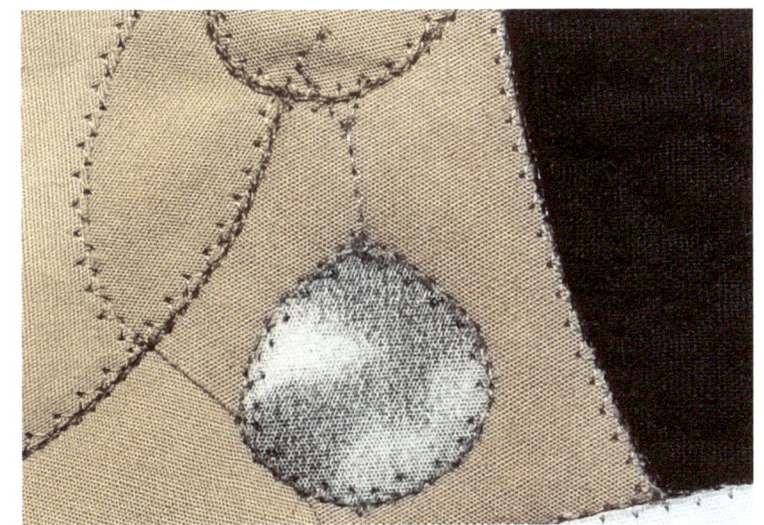

1. On this fabric use the circle template and a pencil to trace ¾ of the way around a 13/16" (20.637 mm) circle.

2. To complete the earring, I removed the template and extended the open part of the circle to make a teardrop shape.

3. Shade in the "pearl" shape with a black coloured pencil (see picture) taking into account that the light is coming from the upper left.

4. Fuse this piece of fabric to another piece of white fabric. This makes sure that the darker colours underneath will not shadow through; as happens when a light piece of fabric is placed on top of a darker one.

5. Once you are happy with your shading, place fusible on the back of the fabric again and cut out the pearl shape and add it to the portrait.

Note: I later stitched in the ring in her ear and the fine chain that holds the pearl.

Now that you have the fabrics in place on your portrait, we will go on to Chapter 5 where you will review your portrait before fusing the fabrics down. Keep up the good work!

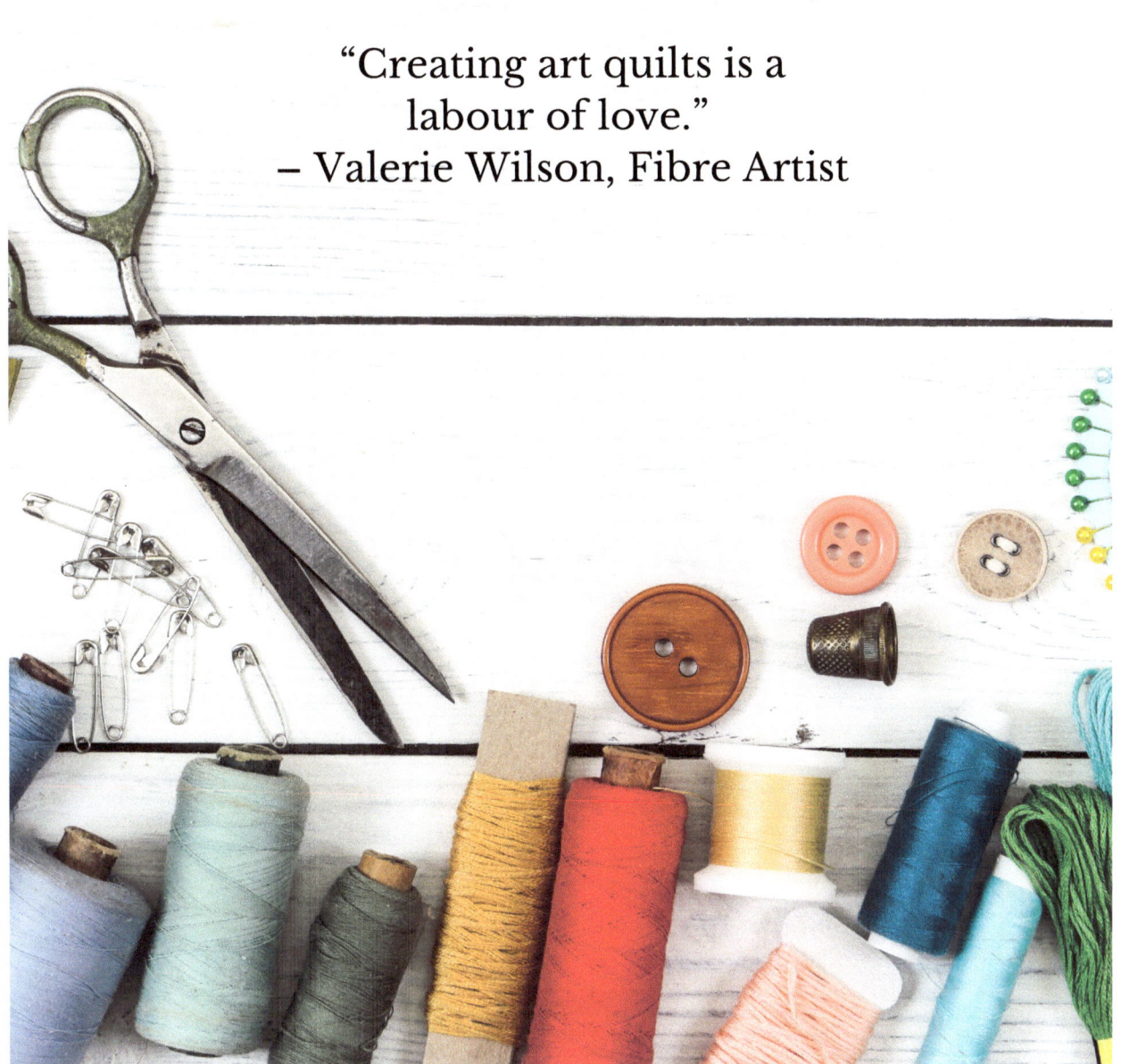

"Creating art quilts is a labour of love."
– Valerie Wilson, Fibre Artist

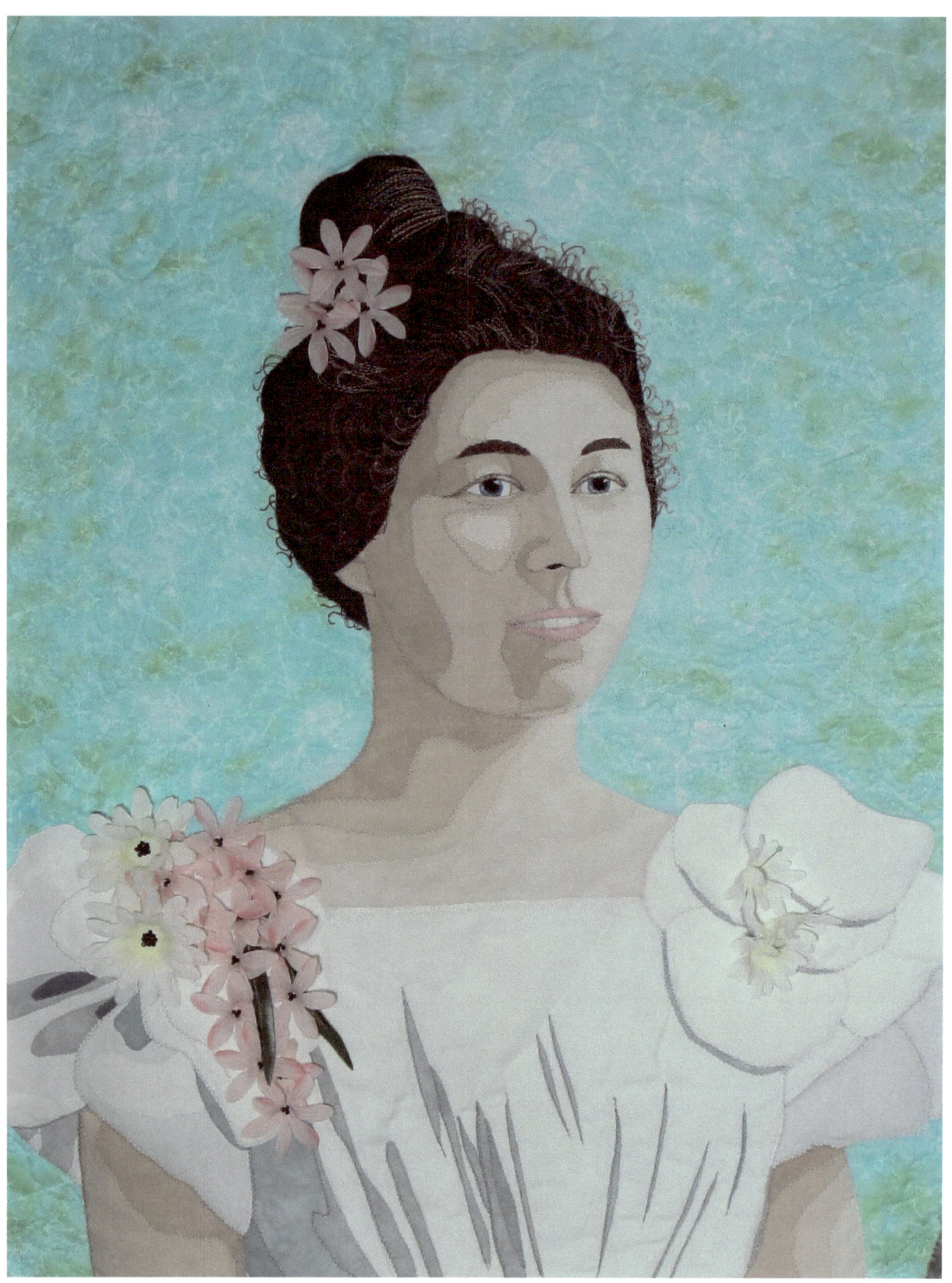

Chapter 5
Reviewing Your Work and Fusing

Are you pleased with what you have done so far? Remember that this is just your first portrait and is a learning experience, your next portrait will be even better.

An important first step before fusing the fabrics down is to carefully look over your portrait to see whether there are any final changes that you might want to make.

Once the portrait is fused, it is nearly impossible to make changes!

How to review your portrait

There are several ways to get a different perspective on your portrait. In all of them, it helps to get a distance away from the portrait. This is not always possible if you have a small quilting area, so here are some suggestions.

- Prop the foam core up, with your portrait on it, and observe it from a distance. If you can't get far enough back in a room, then place the portrait where you can look at it from another spot through the doorway.
- Look at your quilt through a peephole. These are used in doors so that you can see who is standing outside. A version of this tool can often be found in quilting stores or you can get one at a hardware store. This tool gives you a long distance view of any quilt.
- Take a picture with your camera or cell phone and review it on your device.

Any of these methods will help you to get a different view of your portrait and help to identify problem areas if any.

Areas to check:

1. Look closely for any spots where two fabrics did not adequately overlap, leaving thin white lines, where the foundation fabric is showing. These are very difficult to hide but can be remedied relatively easily now by repositioning or replacing some of the fabric pieces. This step requires you to get close to the surface of the portrait and look carefully.

2. Check whether the values in the face and neck look good? There should be a subtle variation between the values so that from a distance the skin looks smooth, not patchy.

3. Does the headdress look as though it has folds in it? (Some detail will be added later with stitching)

4. Do you have the highlights in the eyes in the right position? (see the reference photo in the section on the eyes)

5. Do the eyelids cover the top and bottom edges of the irises?

6. Do you like the way that your pearl looks? Does it look rounded or does the shading need adjustment?

Fusing

Before starting to fuse your portrait, check that the sole plate of the iron is really clean. You don't want to get smudges. There are a variety of iron cleaners available. If you don't have one handy, try dampening a cloth, bunching it up and running the iron over it to see if anything comes off.

Depending on the kind of fusible you are using, follow the directions for fusing the portrait – lifting and placing the iron from section to section (pressing), so that you do not disturb the placement of the pieces.

Pressing 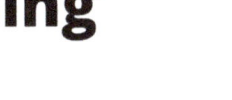 Ironing

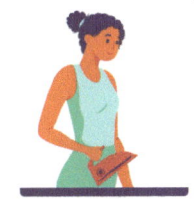

Placing the iron on the fabric.

Leaving it in place for some time.

Lifting it and placing it in another spot.

Sliding the iron across the fabric.

Lite Steam-A-Seam 2® requires steam and a long fusing time (about 20 seconds) in any one spot. I move the iron around a small area at any one time.

Cutting out the portrait

Once the portrait is fused in place, you will cut the portrait out of the foundation fabric.
Cut carefully, close to the face, headscarf and clothing, being careful not to nick the edges of those areas.

Once the portrait is removed from the foundation fabric, you can audition background fabrics.

Choosing the Background

The fabric you choose for the background should not have too much pattern or it will compete with your portrait. I used a solid black fabric for the original version of this portrait.

To audition a background fabric, lay out a large piece of the fabric that you are considering and place the portrait on top of it. See the example below.

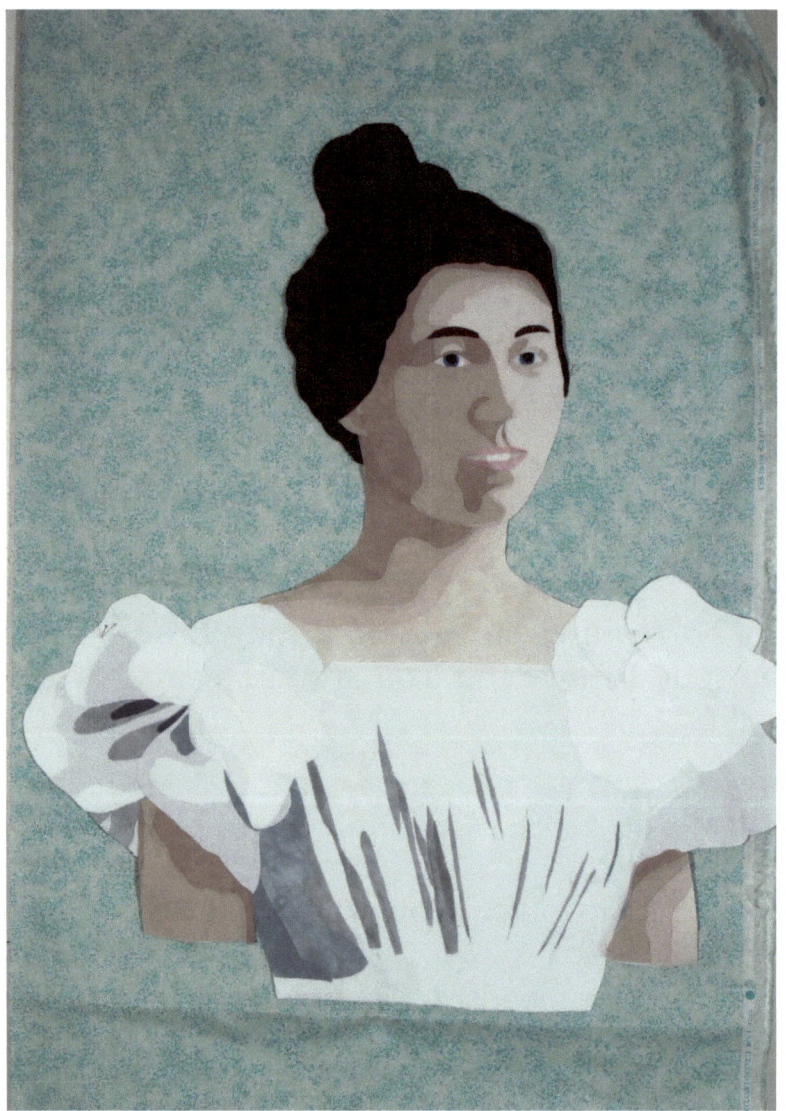

Pro Tip: It is useful to pin the background fabric to the foam core, or design wall, and then pin the portrait on top for a better view. Prop the foam core up so that you can see the portrait as it would look on the wall.

Once you have chosen your background fabric, iron it and cut out a piece that is larger (by a couple of inches on all sides, than the planned finished size of your piece. I used a piece 27" H x 23" W.

1. Lay the background fabric out on your ironing surface with the longest length from top to bottom.

2. Adhere the portrait to the background

Option #1 - Add fusible to the back of your portrait. You can add the fusible just around the edges to reduce the bulk or you can fuse the whole portrait to the background. You can use any fusible for this step. My suggestion would be to use a light fusible such as Misty Fuse, to reduce the bulk.

Option #2 - Another alternative is to use fabric glue. Carefully lift the edge of the portrait, a bit at a time and place small dots of glue underneath the edges to hold the portrait in place.

The woman is offset toward the right side of the background.

3. If using fusible, fuse the portrait to the background. It is a good idea to fuse from the back, and the front, as there are several layers of fabric.

4. If you want a border, the time to add it is now.

Plain (or butted) Borders

1. Lay your quilt top out flat.

2. Measure vertically top to bottom at 3 places – the 2 sides and the middle. You will use the shortest measurement for the length of the borders. Record this measurement.

Measuring the quilt top before adding the borders helps to ensure that the quilt top will be even on each side.

Note: directional fabric will be best cut with the design on the fabric all pointing in the same direction. This will mean some border fabric will be cut across the width of the fabric and some cut lengthwise.

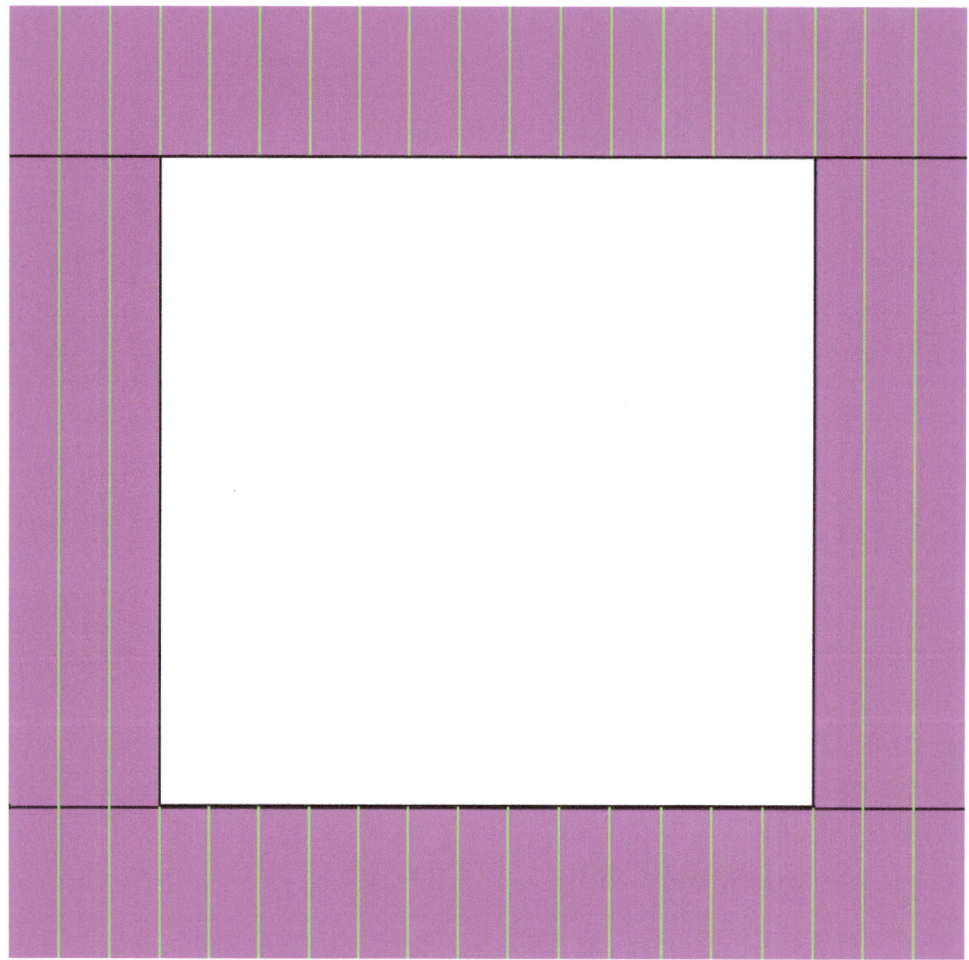

3. Using the length of the quilt top, a measurement you previously recorded, cut the side border strips. Remember to add a ½" extra (1/4" for each side) on the side of the border for seam allowances. E.g. For a 4" border, you would cut 4 ½" wide strips.

4. If you need to join pieces of fabric to get the correct length, allow extra fabric for a mitred join. You will need the size of the width of the border added to the length you measured for your border, to allow for the mitre.

For example, if you have a 5" wide border (cut 5 ½") and a quilt top that measures 72" in length, you will need to cut your side border pieces so that you have 72 + 5 ½" = 79 1/2" in length to allow for the join.

5. Fold the border fabric in half (end to end) and mark the centre with a pin. With the border laid out flat, fold one end to meet the pin in the centre. Put a pin in to mark the fold. Repeat with the other end of the border.

6. Place pins in your quilt top to mark it in the same way.

7. With fabrics right sides together, match the pins at the middle of the border and quilt top, and then the ones on each side and pin in place. Line up the outer edge of the quilt top to the outer edge of the border. Pin in place.

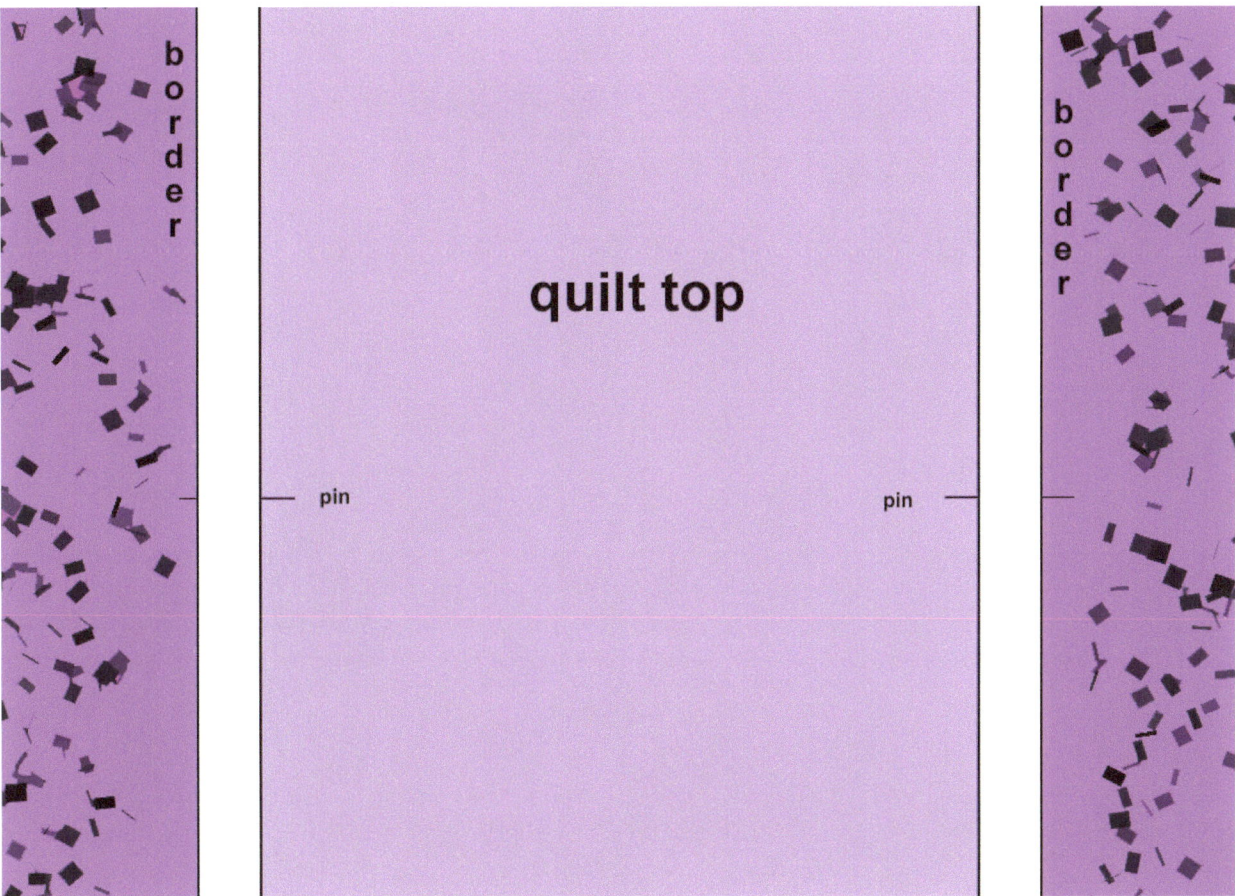

8. Working in sections, pin at intervals easing in any fullness.

9. Sew the borders to the sides of the quilt with a ¼" seam allowance.

Note: If there is more fullness in the quilt top than the border, sew the seam with the quilt top down against the feed dogs and use a regular sewing foot (not a walking foot). This will help to ease in the fullness.

10. Press the seams towards the borders.

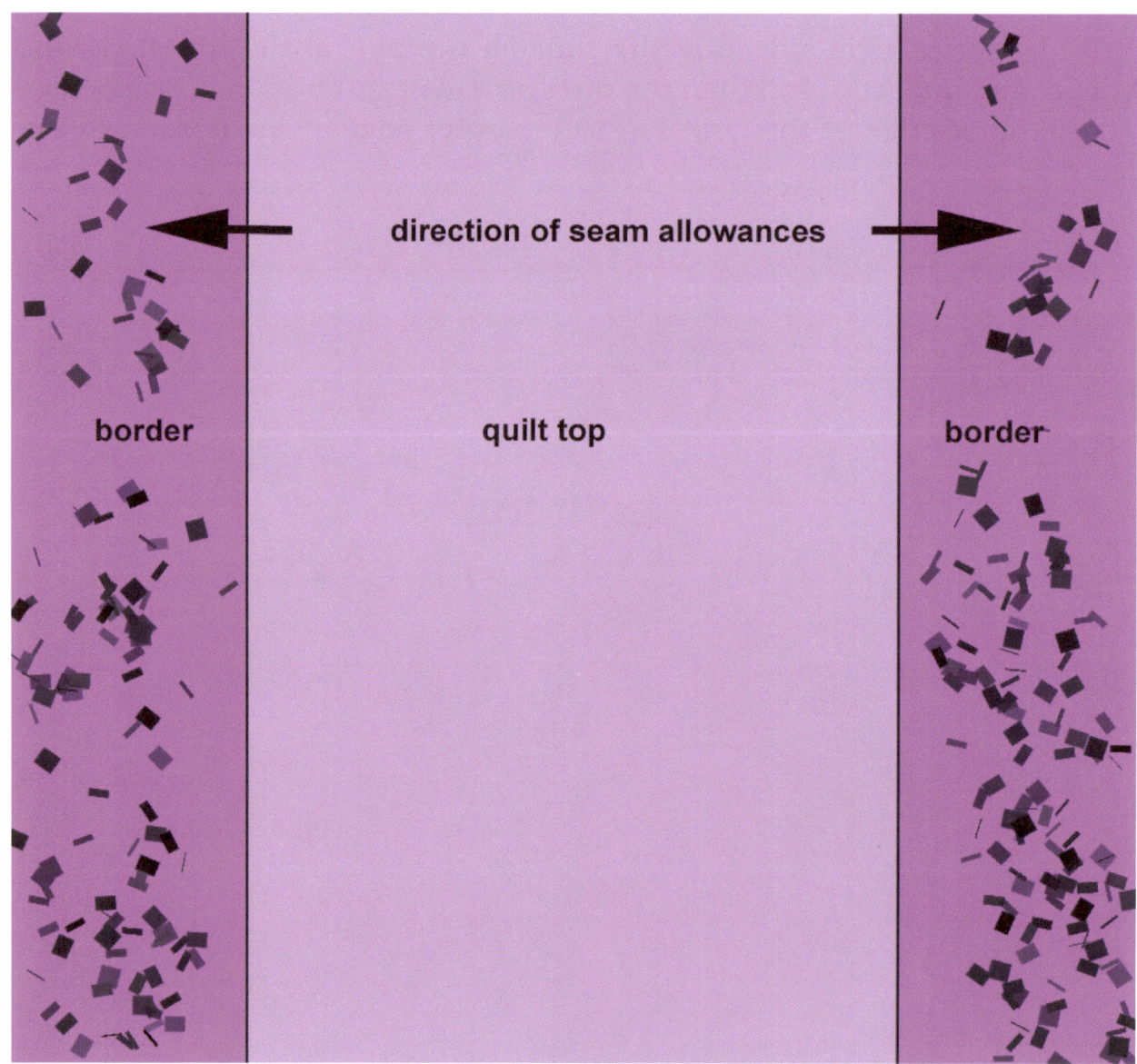

11. Measure across the width of the quilt top including the borders at 3 places - the top, middle and bottom.

12. Once again, using the shortest measurement cut your top and bottom borders.

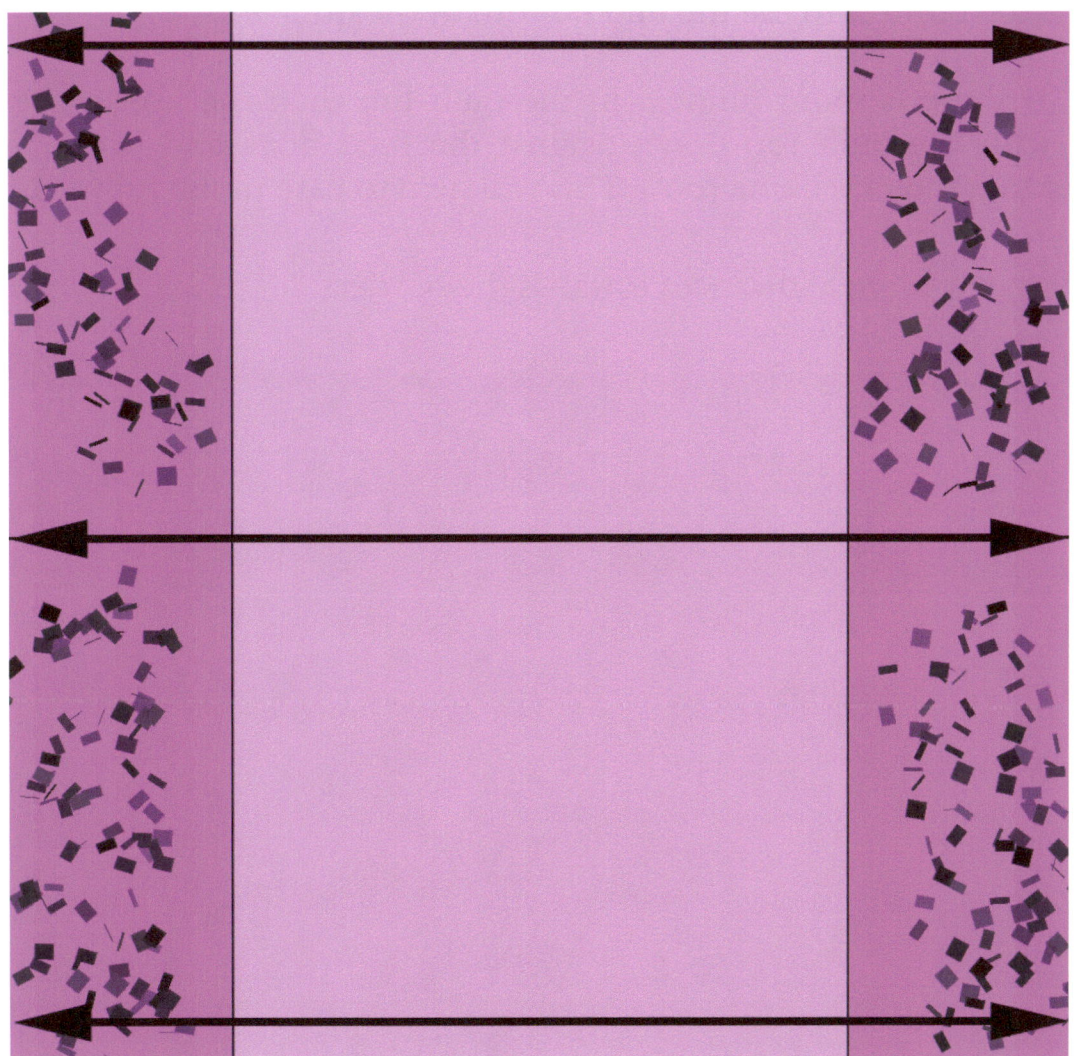

13. Fold the border fabric in half and mark the centre with a pin. With the border laid out flat, fold one end to meet the pin in the centre. Put a pin in to mark the fold. Repeat with the other end of the border.

14. Repeat this same process with your quilt top.

15. With the fabrics right sides together, match the pins at the middle and on each side and pin in place. Line up the outer edge of the quilt to the outer edge of the border. Pin in place.

16. Working in sections, pin at intervals easing in any fullness.

17. Sew the borders to the top and bottom of the quilt with a 1/4" seam.

Note: If there is more fullness in the quilt top than the border, sew the seam with the quilt top down against the feed dogs and use a regular sewing foot (not a walking foot). This will help to ease in the fullness.

18. Press the seam allowances towards the borders.

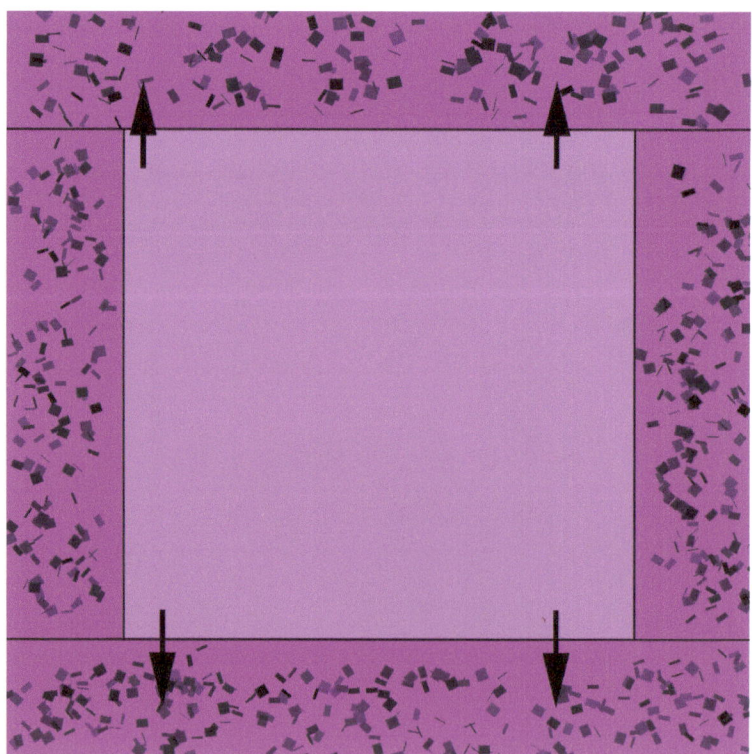

Your borders are finished!

Now it is time for the detail stitching that will add life to your portrait.

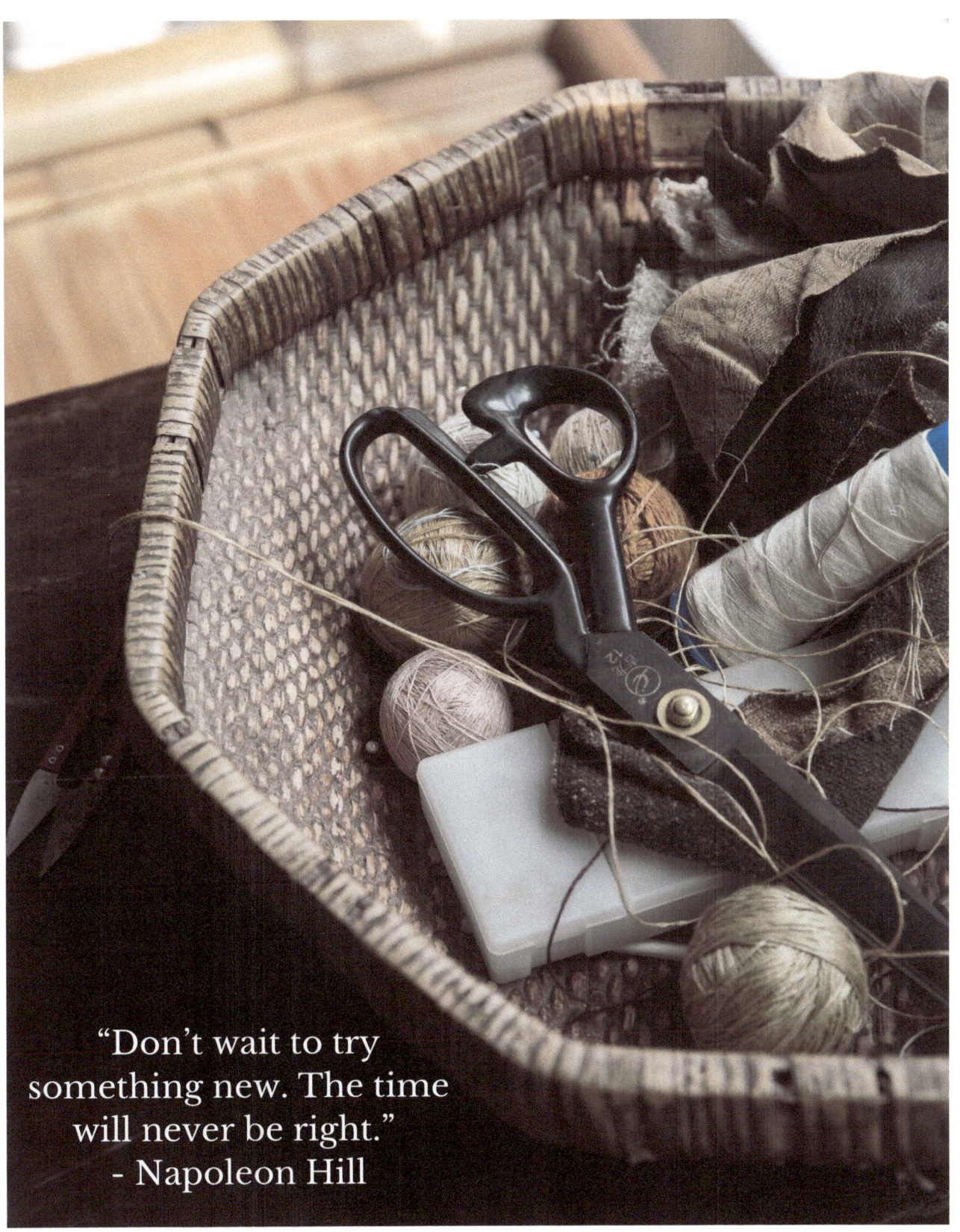

"Don't wait to try something new. The time will never be right."
- Napoleon Hill

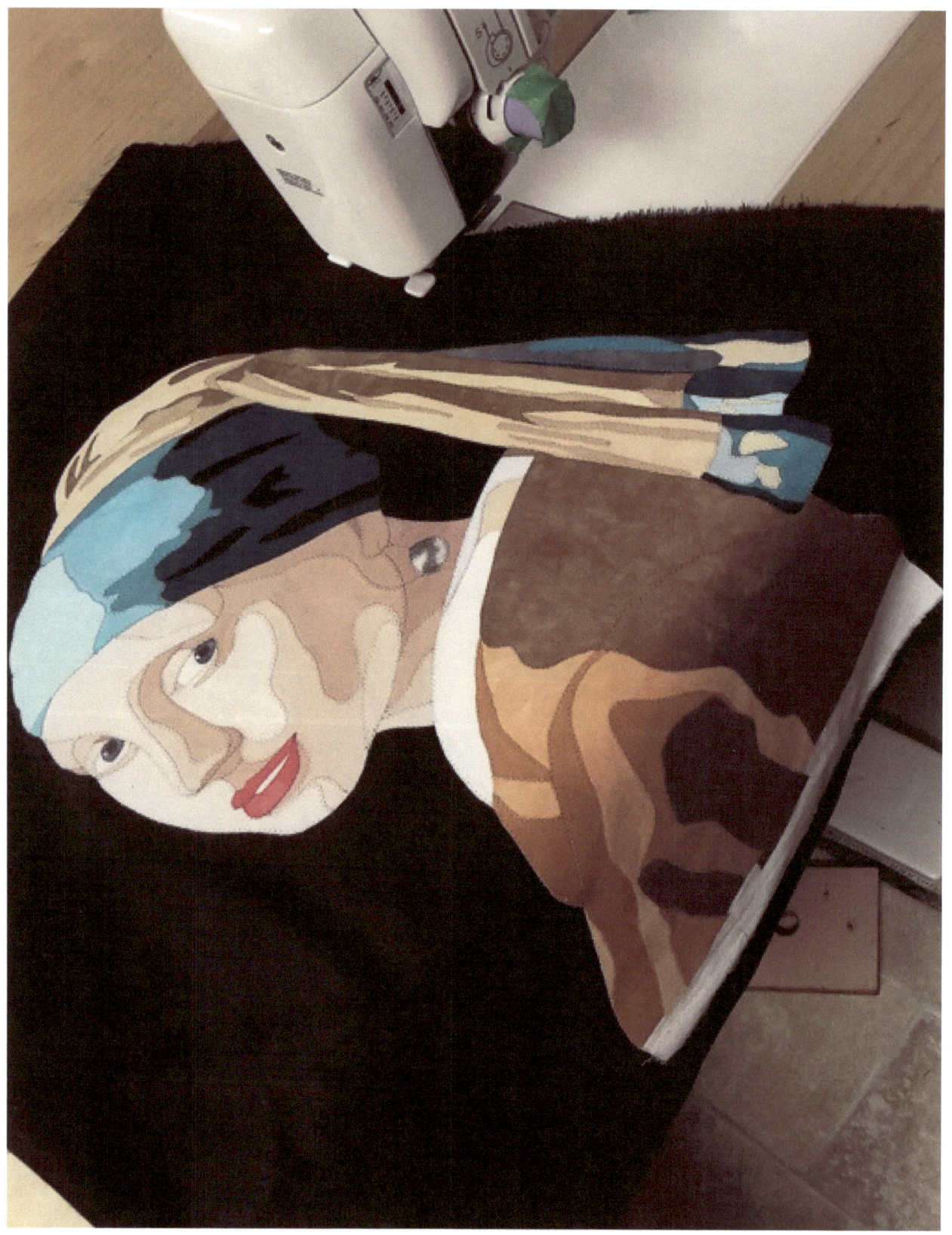

Chapter 6
Stitching and Adding Detail

Edge Stitching

You have made good progress. Now is the time to secure all the edges of the fabric pieces and then add some essential detail stitching to bring out her features and add interest to her head scarf and gown.

Threads

You can use clear monofilament as the top thread when stitching the face and clothing, to avoid having to change threads. If you decide to use this type of thread, I recommend Superior's Monopoly as it is polyester, not nylon, and is very fine. It is also, not as shiny as some other monofilament threads and will not melt when ironed (as will nylon thread). I suggest you lower the top tension on your sewing machine when using monofilament thread.

My personal choice is to use finer weight threads (cotton, silk or polyester) – 60 WT to 100 WT for most of the edge stitching.

I have done portraits using all 50 WT threads which look fine too. Test and see what will work best for you.

I do use 50 WT threads for the detail stitching.

Thread weights

The numbering system for threads gives a larger number to a finer thread and a smaller number to a thicker thread. Thus, a 100 WT thread is very fine, while a 40 WT thread is thicker and heavier. The best way to compare thread weights is by feel and sight as there are variations between brands and threads.

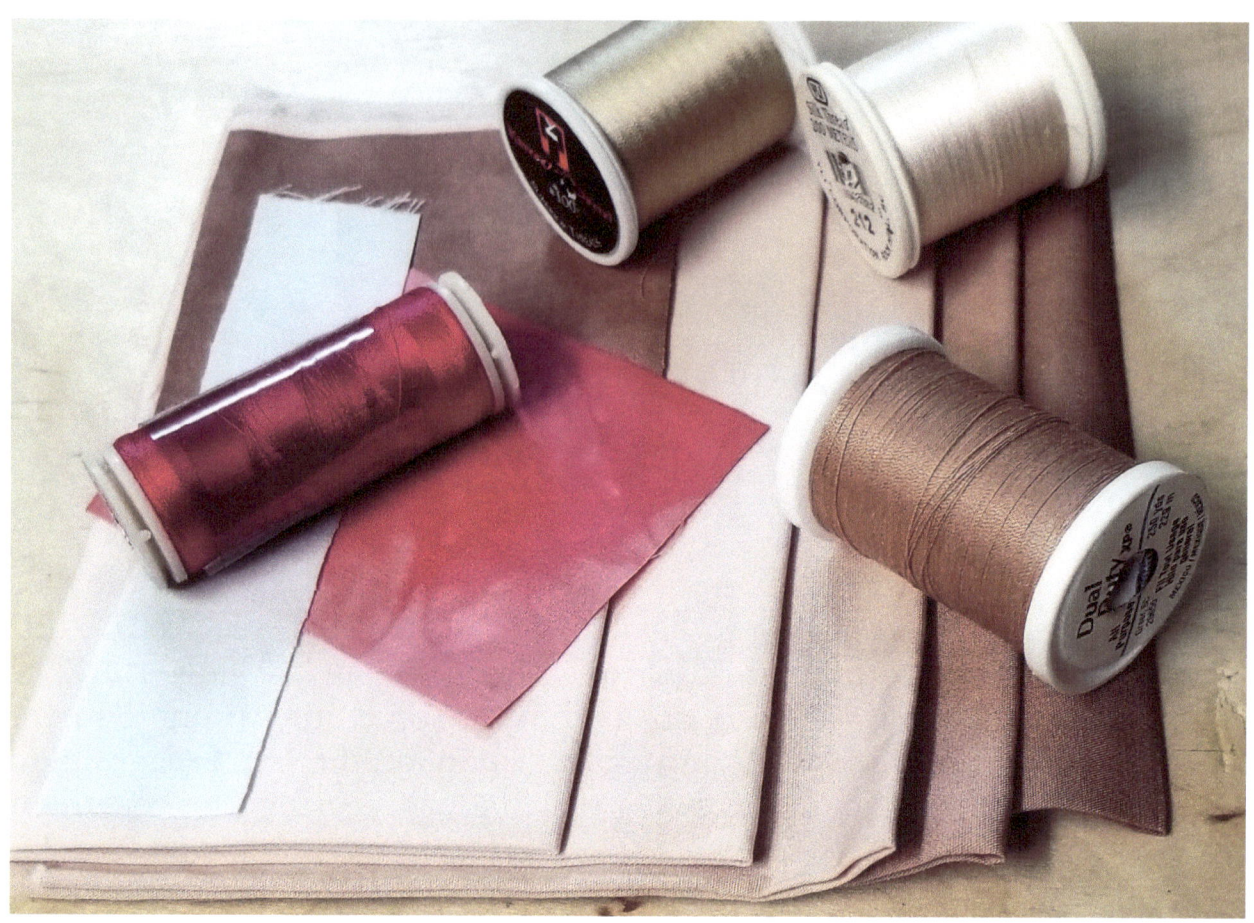

Suggestions for threads:

Fine weight threads: Invisafil or DecoBob by Wonderfil, Bottom Line or MicroQuilter by Superior Threads and 100 WT silk threads by YLI and Kimono silk by Superior threads.

Other threads (50 WT) – Gutterman, Mettler, So Fine and Masterpiece by Superior Threads, Efina by Wonderfil. Aurifil, Coats and Clark thread.

Match the threads as closely as possible to the colour of the fabric you are sewing. It saves time if you sew all one value of a colour at the same time, so you don't have to change threads as often.

I look for the colour match I want and use cotton, cotton/poly or polyester threads.

Needles

I use a Topstitch needle which has a sharp point and a larger eye and works well with a variety of threads. If you are interested in learning more about needles, there is a reference to an article on needle types in the Resource section at the back of the book.

The needle size you use in your sewing machine should match the thread weight that you are using. So, if you are sewing with a 50 WT thread, you should be using a 80/12 or 75/11 needle size. If you are sewing with a thread like Bottom Line (60 WT) or Invisafil (100 WT), I would recommend a 70/10 size needle.

Pro tip: Change your needle after 30 hours of sewing or after every project. The needle tip wears down microscopically. A worn needle can lead to poor tension and skipped stitches.

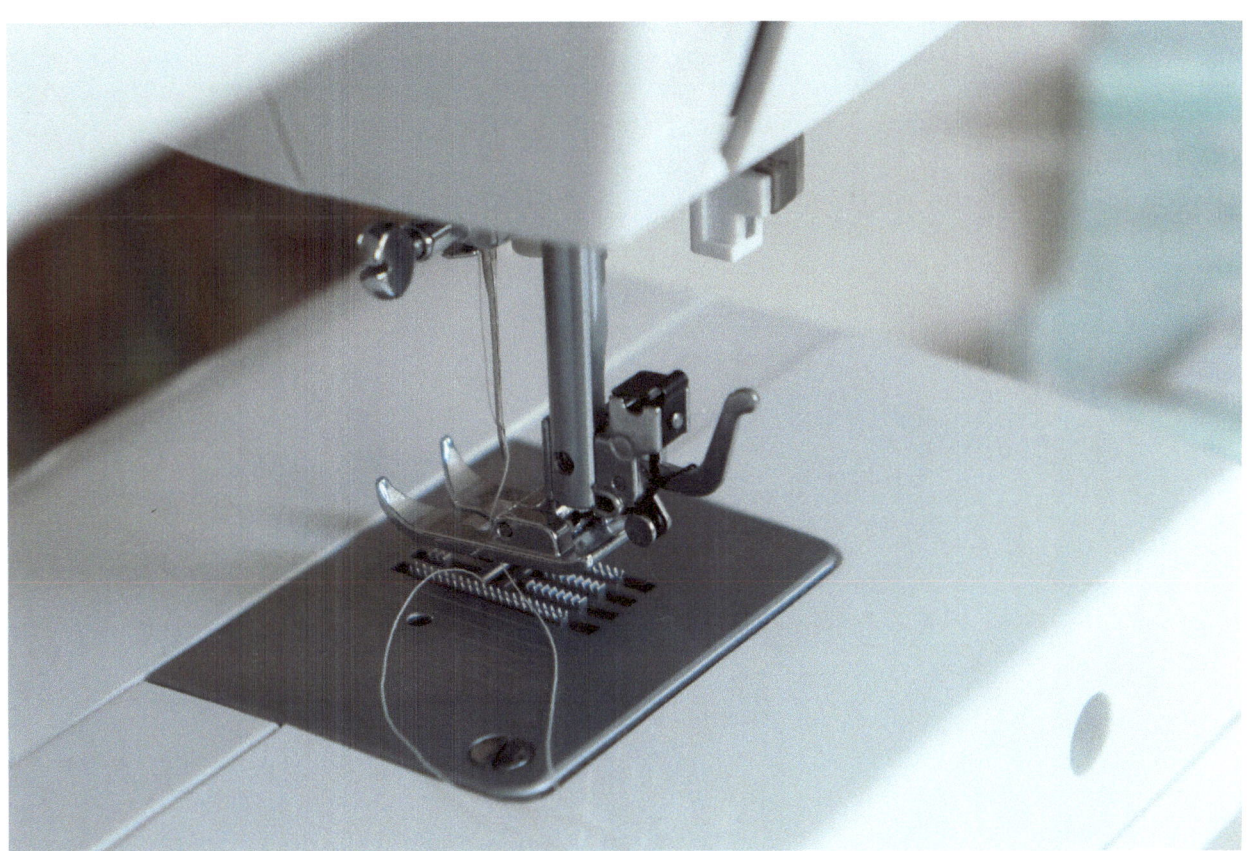

Stitching the fabric pieces in place

Hopefully, you saved some scraps of your fabric, and have them handy, to test out your thread colours, stitch length and width and sewing machine tension.

Note: I use a .80 to 1.25 stitch width on my sewing machine. Practise on some scrap fabric and see what width works best for you on your machine.

Zigzag stitch around the edges of all the fabric shapes using an open toe foot or regular sewing foot on your sewing machine.

If you have problems with "pop-ups" (bobbin thread showing in between the stitches), you may want to change bobbin colours to match the top thread.

Don't worry about a mess of threads on the back, as these won't be seen later.

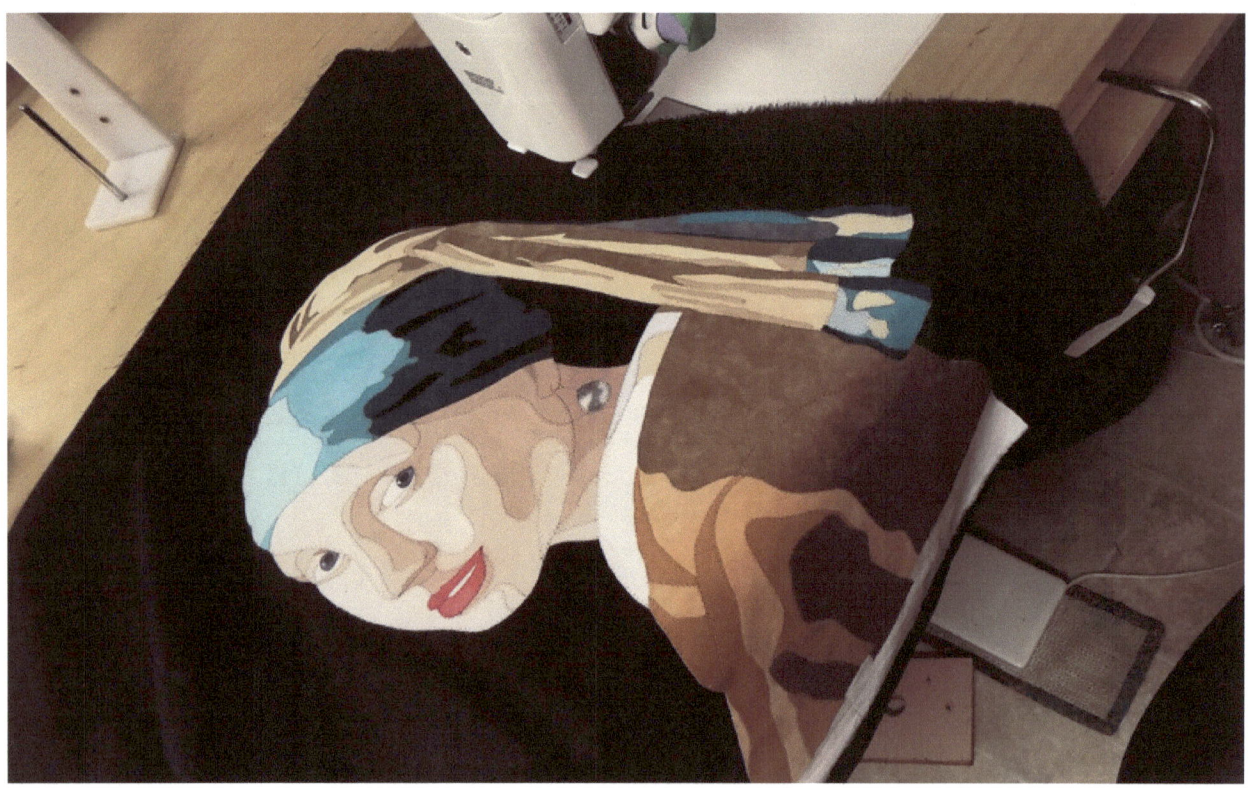

Detail Stitching

Use 50 WT threads so that the detail stitching will show and add interest.

Eyes:

a. Stitch in the eyelid crease with a narrow zigzag stitch and a darker shade of thread. This helps to round the look of the eye.

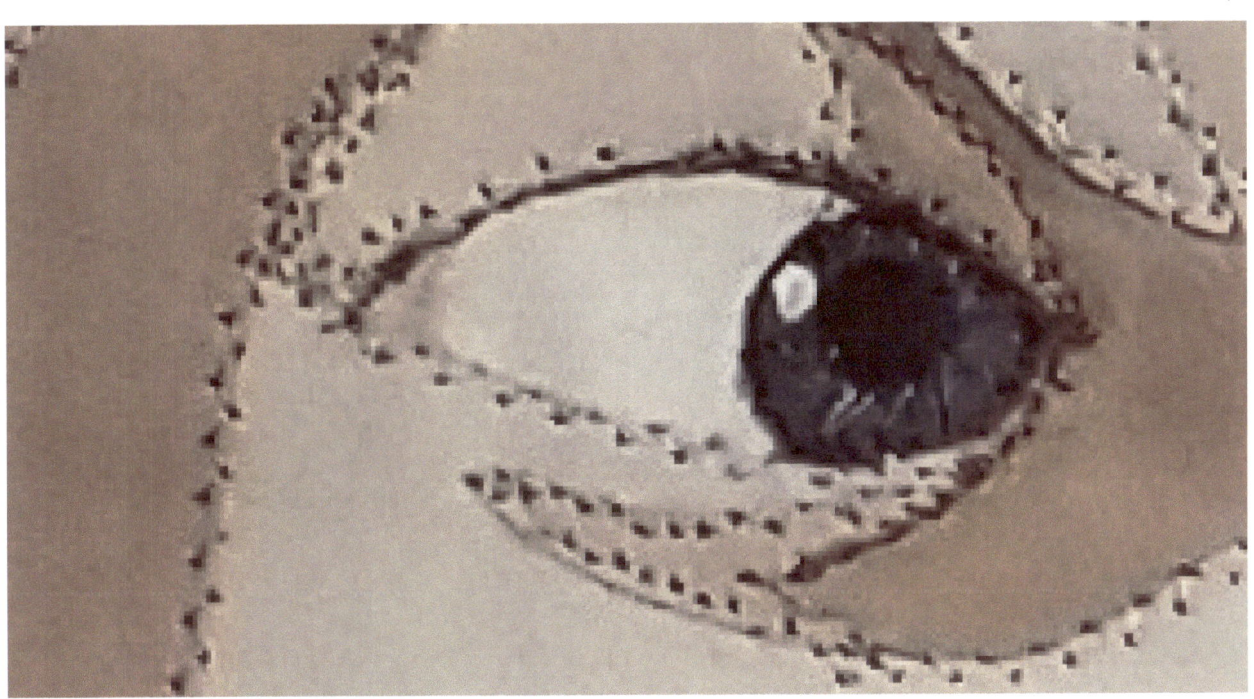

b. Stitch along the upper edges of the eyelids with a straight stitch and a darker thread. I double stitched the outer edge of each eye to create more shadow.

Iris:

Create dimension in the iris.
a. You can create a zigzag look one stitch at a time with your sewing machine by rotating the portrait as you go and doing one stitch at a time by manually turning the fly wheel. These lines radiate out and around the pupil.

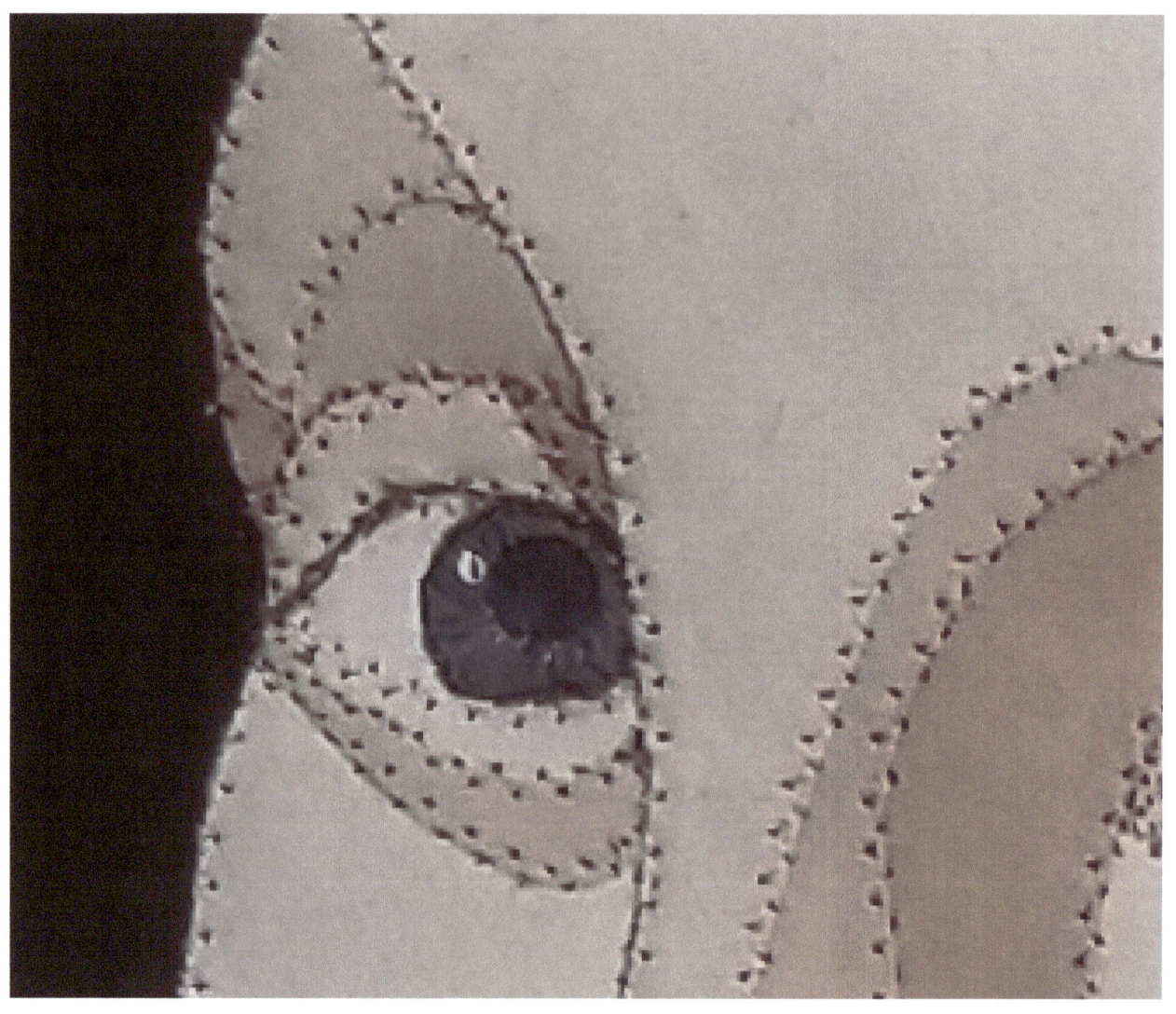

b. Gel pens can be used for this purpose as well. It is best to test them on a scrap of the same fabric as the iris, before trying them on your portrait.

c. Look for the highlight in the eye in your photo. If you did not use paint in the beginning the highlight can be added by free motion stitching with white thread.

d. Adding highlights helps to make the eyes look real and the person alive. Both highlights will be on the same sides of the eyeballs (in this case both on the right side of the eyes at the edge of the iris.). You can also hand stitch the highlight in the eyes.

Nose:

Use a darker thread, with a straight stitch, to stitch around the bottom of the nose. This creates depth and shadow.

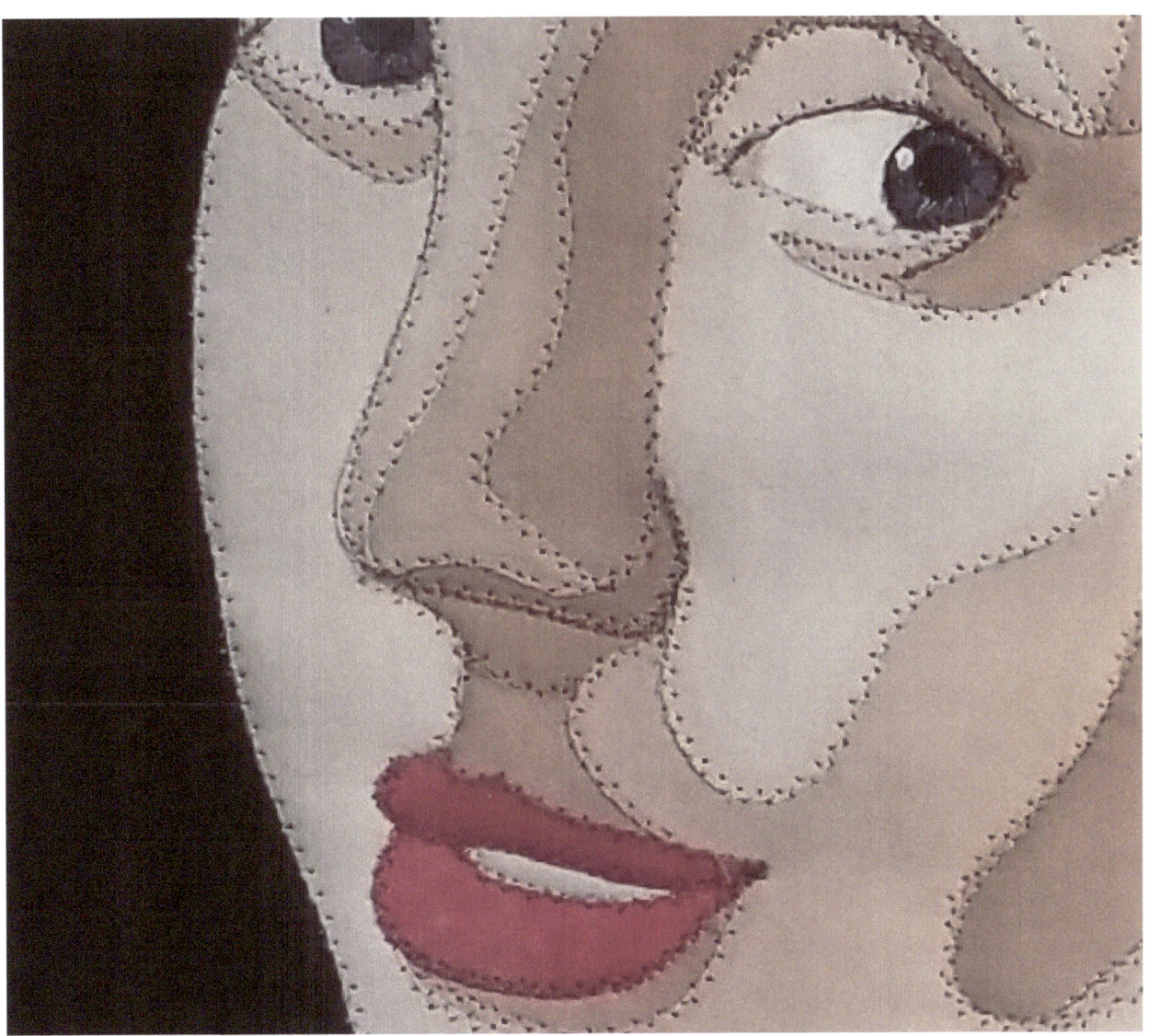

Lips:

Stitch a darker line below each lip to help create a more rounded look. To create the highlight on the lower lip, if needed, use a white coloured pencil to add it.

Chin/neck/ear:

Stitch a darker line, using a straight line or a zigzag stitch, under the chin. This helps to distinguish the neck from the throat and adds a slight shadow. See picture. Also, stitch a darker line on the side of the face between the face and the ear.

Where the neckline of her dress meets the neck, you may want to add a little shadow on the neck (zigzag stitch with darker thread) to create depth and shadow.

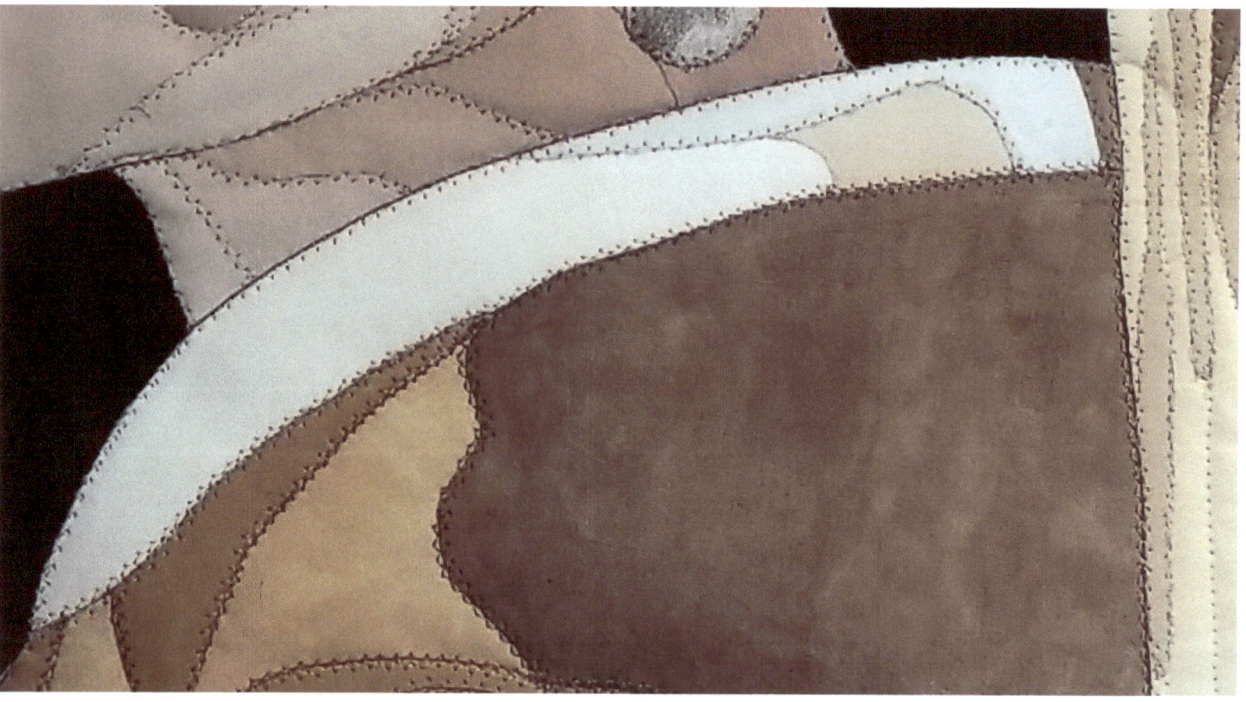

Congratulations you have done it! Now prop your portrait up and see how the detail stitching makes her look more alive.

Now on to the next chapter where we will discuss quilting your portrait.

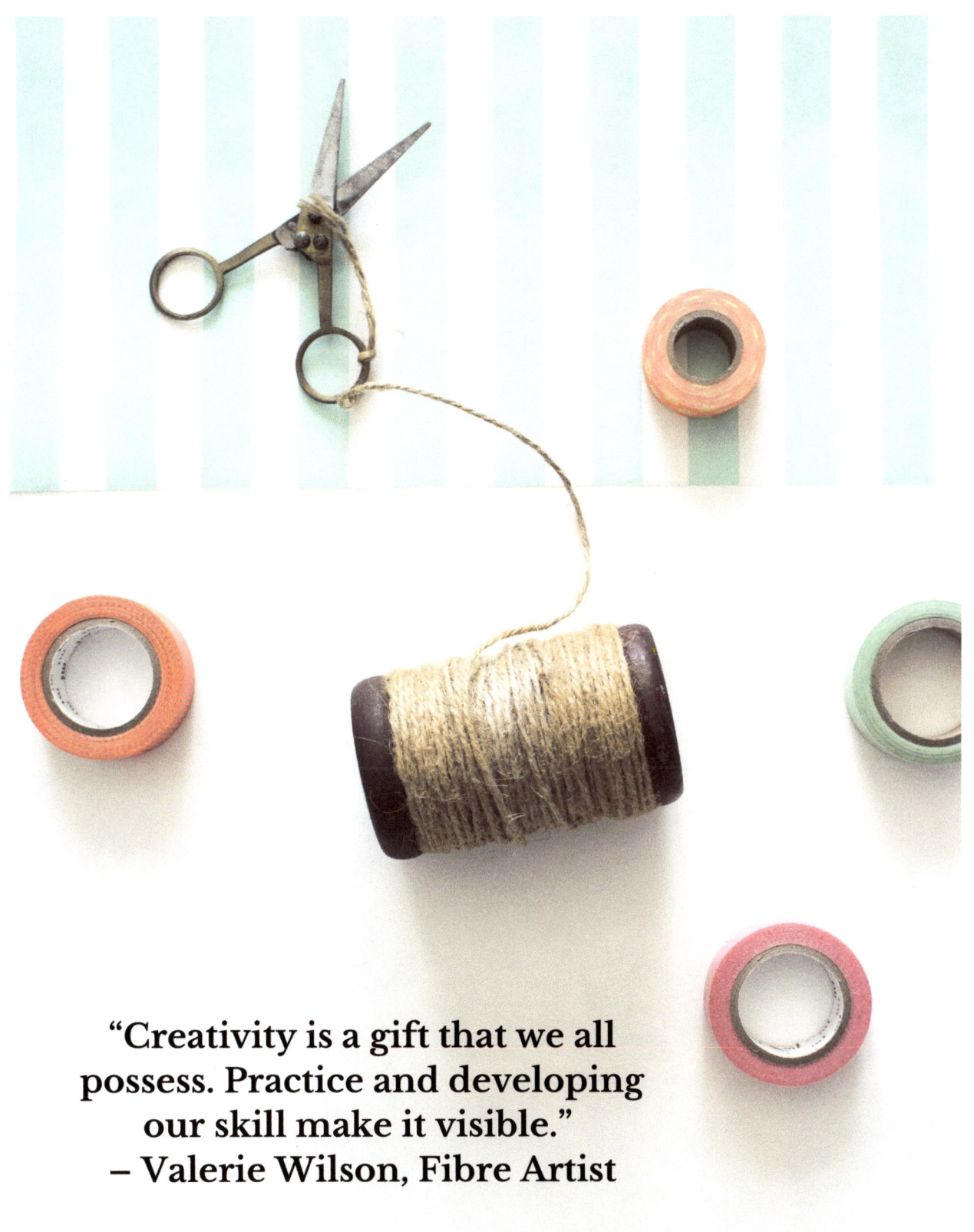

"Creativity is a gift that we all possess. Practice and developing our skill make it visible."
– Valerie Wilson, Fibre Artist

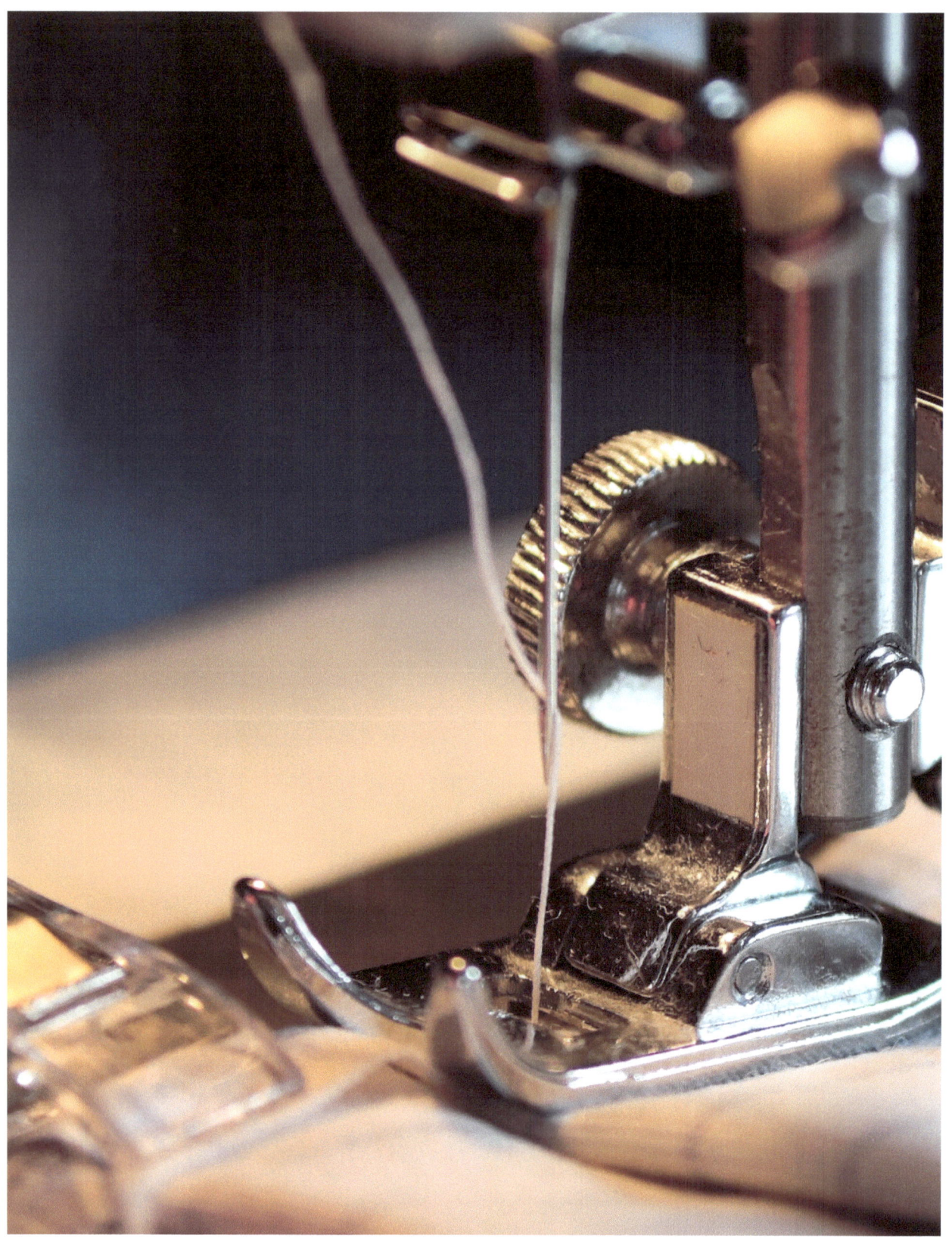

Chapter 7
Quilting Your Portrait

The quilting you add to your portrait will give it even more dimension. I do minimal quilting on my portraits but the density of quilting used is a personal choice.

Pro Tip: If you are feeling nervous about quilting your portrait, I have a special method that will allow you to try quilting your portrait, without actually stitching on it!

To try this method, do the following:

a. Either scan your portrait (maybe just the face and neck area) into your computer or take a picture of it with your digital camera.
b. Print the portrait onto fabric at its actual size. You can buy sheets specially prepared for printing with an inkjet printer. The colours may not print true, but this is not a problem as this exercise is only designed to check your quilting.
c. Layer and quilt the printed image.
d. If you are happy with the results, then go on to quilt your actual portrait.

Preparing the quilt for quilting

Layer the portrait as follows:

1. Place the backing fabric face down. Be sure to iron this fabric so it is nice and smooth.
2. Add the batting on top of the backing fabric and smooth it carefully.
3. Place your portrait face up on top.
4. Secure the layers either with pin basting or hand basting.

You will need to pull out any basting threads just before you stitch over them. I usually only pin in the background, unless I am creating a full figure portrait, at which point I will add pins in the clothing, etc. but not the face. I like to avoid pinholes in the face. They are hard to get rid of due to the fusible used.

Some quilters like to use fusible sprays to hold the layers together. Be sure to follow the directions for these sprays and use them in a well-ventilated area (preferably outside). Watch for overspray which can make surrounding surfaces very sticky.

Thread Choices

For the quilting on the face, you can use clear monofilament thread at the top or you can change the colours of your thread to match the area that you are quilting. It is your choice.

If you choose to use monofilament thread, be sure it is polyester and not nylon. The nylon thread is thicker and stiffer, and harder to use.

Some use monofilament thread in the bobbin as well. I do not. Monofilament thread is a bit slippery and works well with regular thread. However, it does not grip itself well and can cause tension issues and skipped stitches.

If using coloured thread for the quilting, you may want to also use that same colour of thread in the bobbin. This helps to avoid tiny dots of another thread colour showing on the top of the quilt.

The different colours of thread on the back will blend into a busy looking fabric or create an interesting pattern on a plainer fabric.

Pro Tip: Always test your thread choices on a scrap quilting sandwich to be sure that the tension is balanced and nothing is popping up on the top or the bottom.

Quilting

1. Quilt the face mainly in the areas where you stitched previously (when you were using a darker value of thread):

- In the eyelid crease and just above the eye

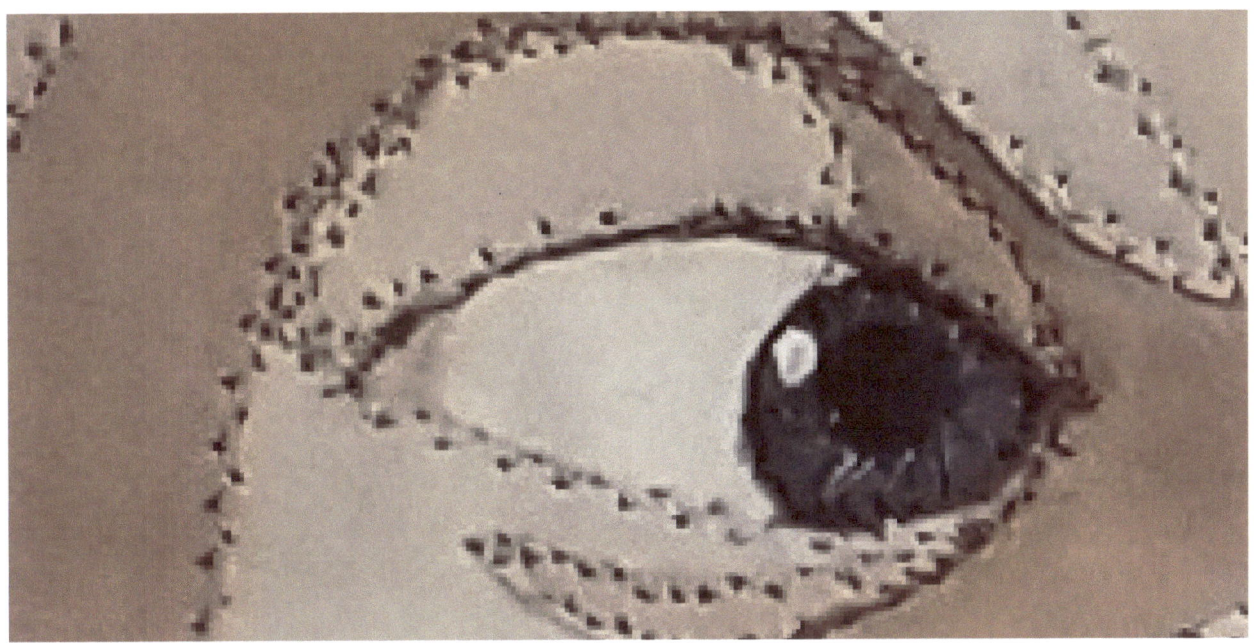

- Between the lips and around the lower lip

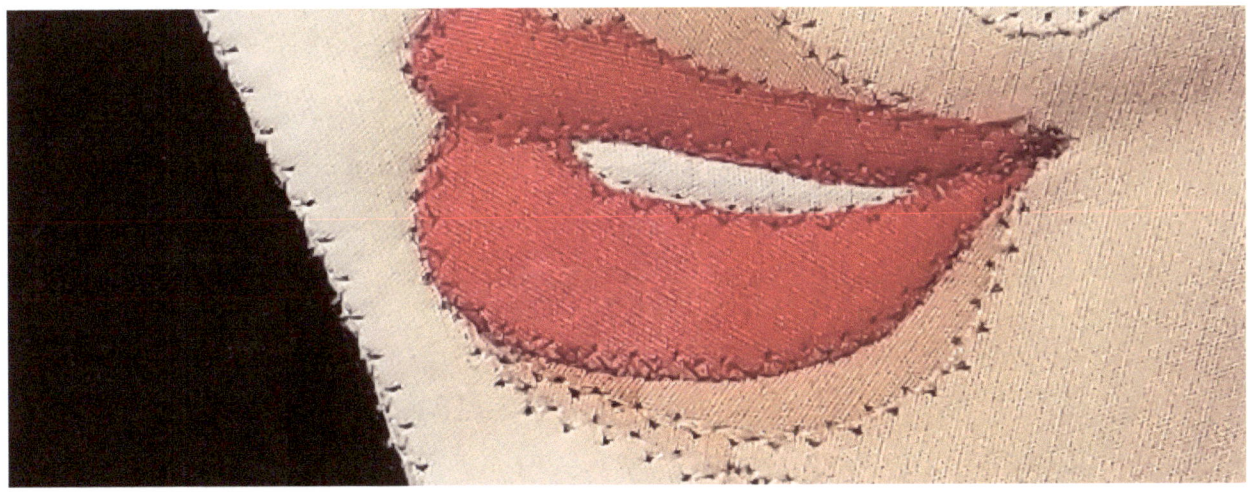

- Around the bottom of the nose and along the left side of the nose

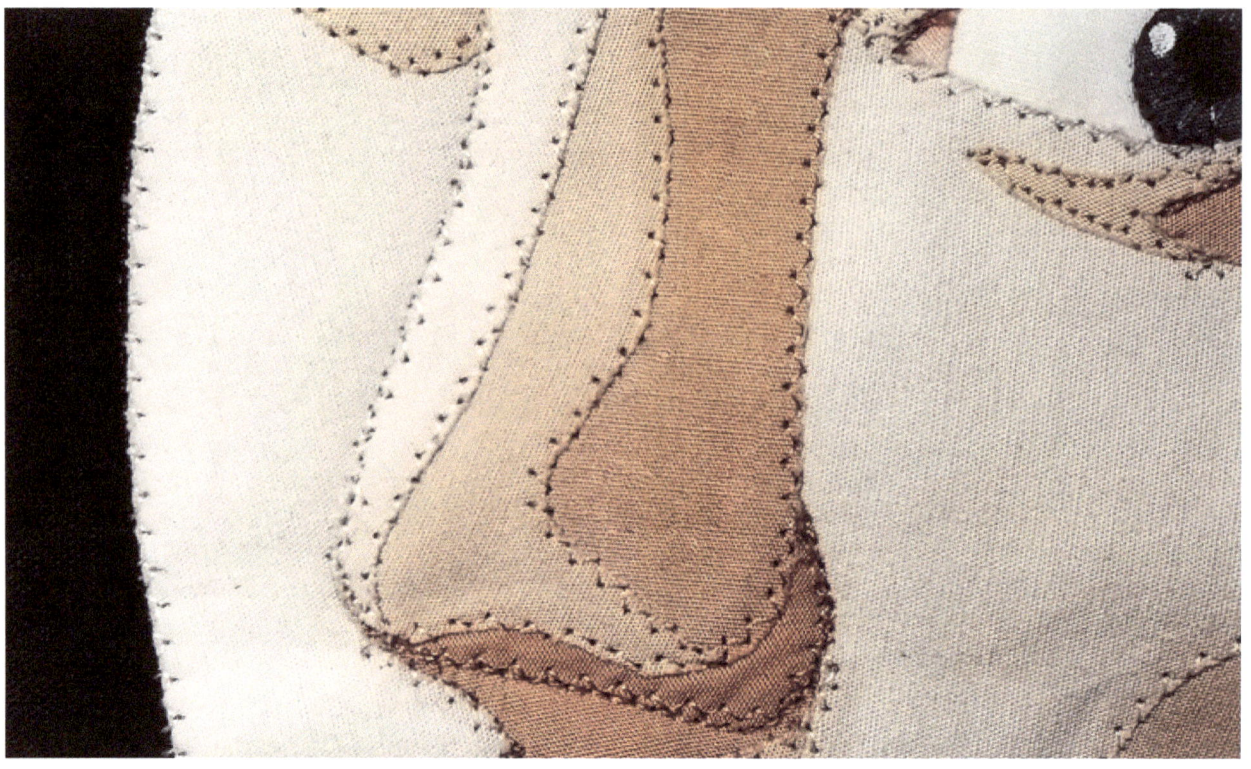

- Just above the collar on the neck and around the pearl

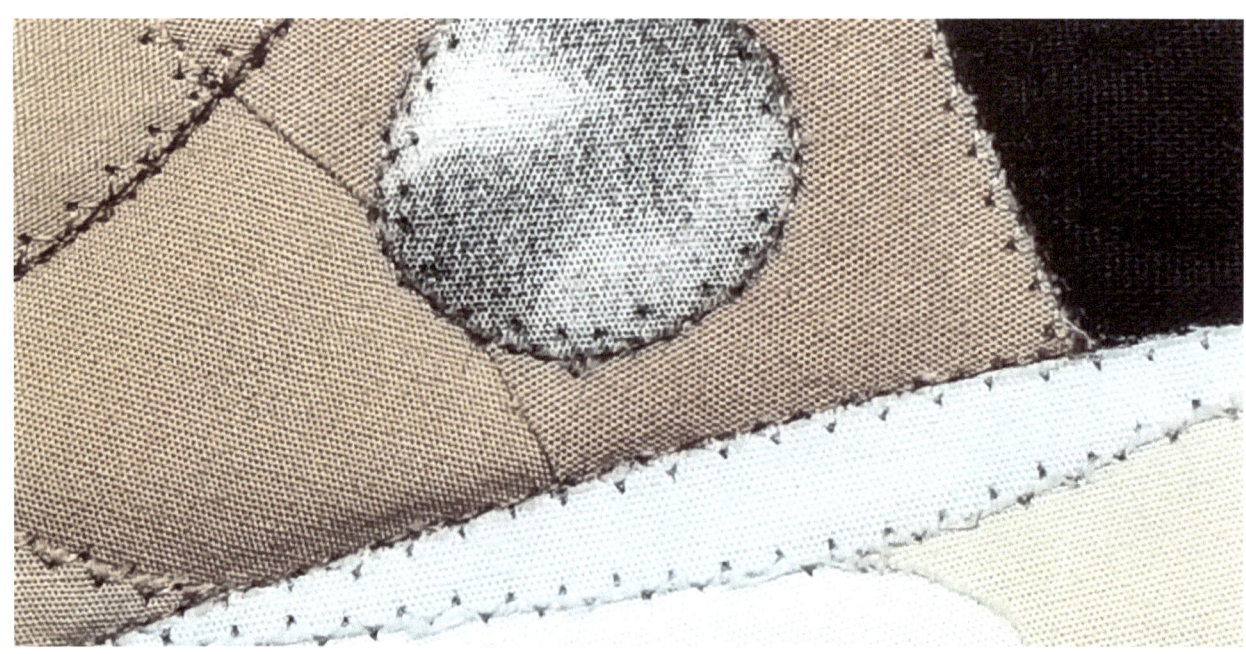

Pro Tip: Note: If you are using monofilament thread, you may want to change to smoke coloured monofilament for darker areas of the portrait as the clear will create a glimmer on dark fabrics.

2. Stitch around the outside of the face including between the face and the ear and around the ear.

3. Stitch around the edges of the headscarf, the major sections of the scarf, and in the creases.

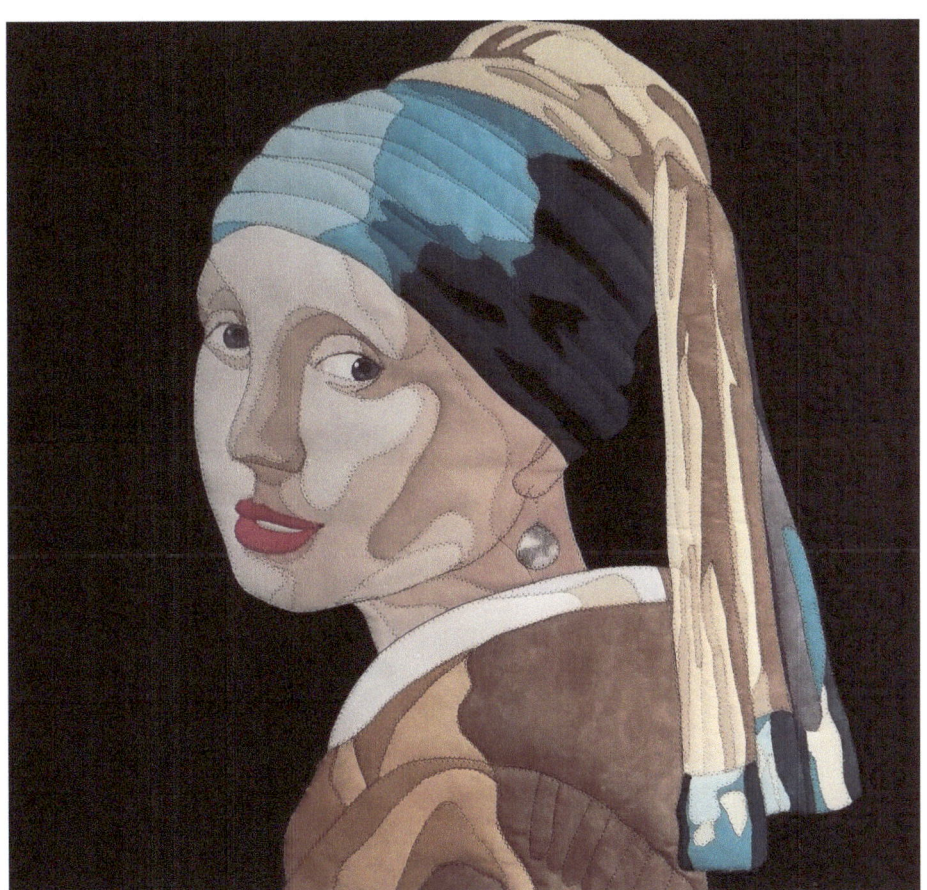

There are curved lines in the headscarf. Look for the indents at the start of the folds in the top part of her headscarf. You can add marking lines with a white marking pencil so you know how the curves should look and that will give you a guide for the quilting. Add some additional lines of quilting here, to give the scarf some more irregular folds.

4. Quilting the gown
- Quilt between the collar and the gown
- Along the outside edges of the gown
- Along the shoulder seam

You can also quilt around some of the shapes in the gown to add dimension if so desired. I added some detail with my quilting on the back of the shoulder of her gown to add interest.

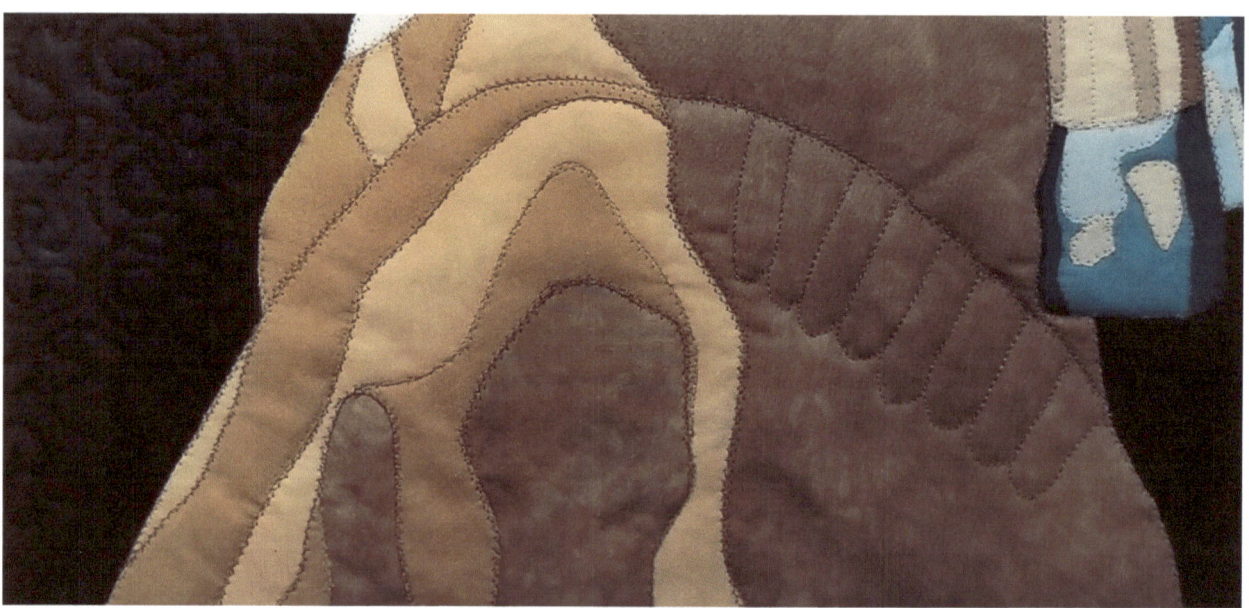

5. Quilt the background with a pattern of your choice. Choose something that will complement the look of your portrait.

Be careful to avoid a dense background design, as it may distort your portrait. If you don't want to do free-motion quilting, look for a quilting design that uses straight lines. Melissa Marginet's book, Walking Foot Quilting Designs, has lots of inspiration.

6. Finally quilt the border, if you have added one.

In the next chapter, I will be discussing how to block your quilt. This is a technique is used to ensure that your quilt will hang nice and flat on the wall.

"Develop a passion for learning. If you do you will never cease to grow."
– Anthony D'Angelo

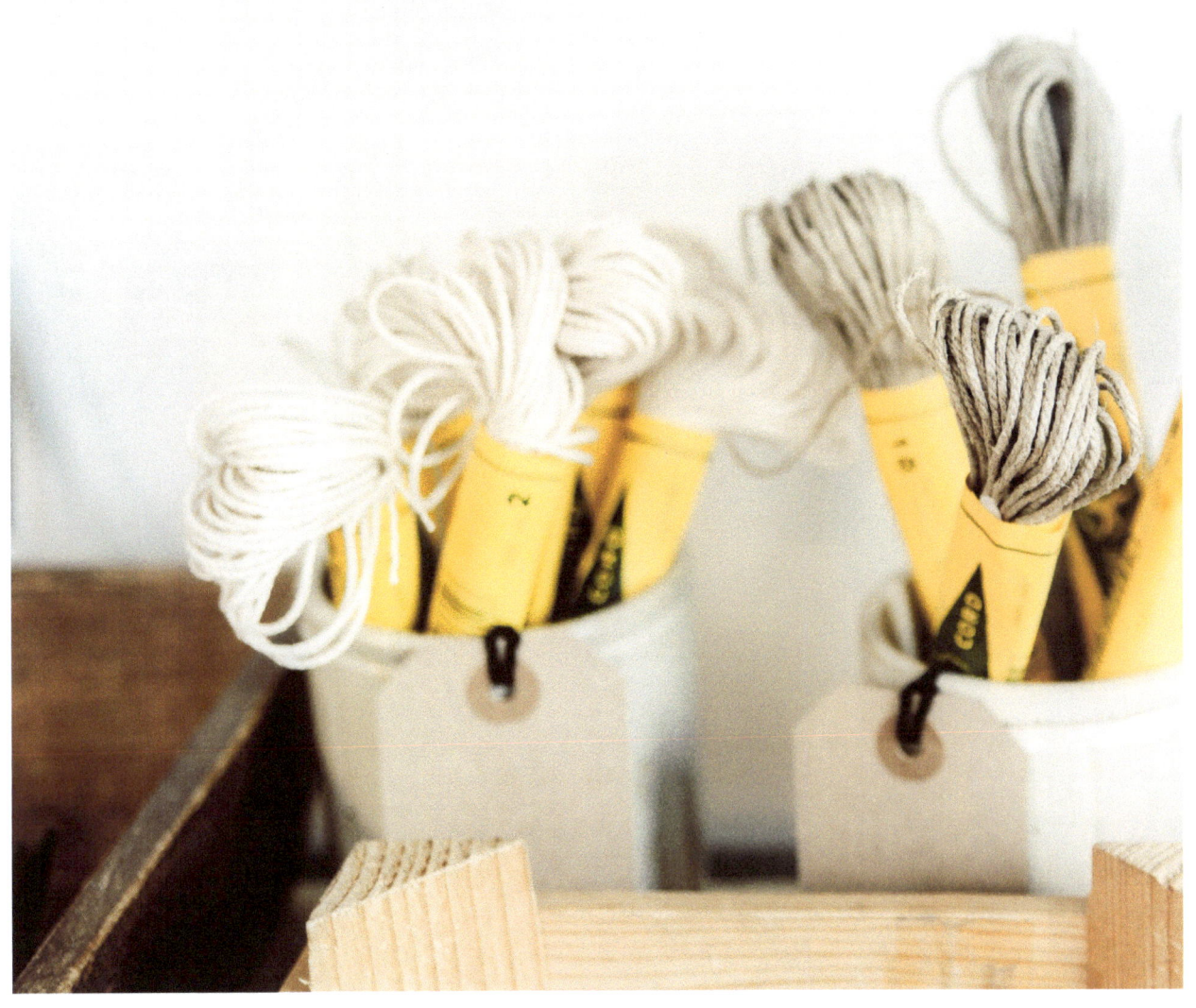

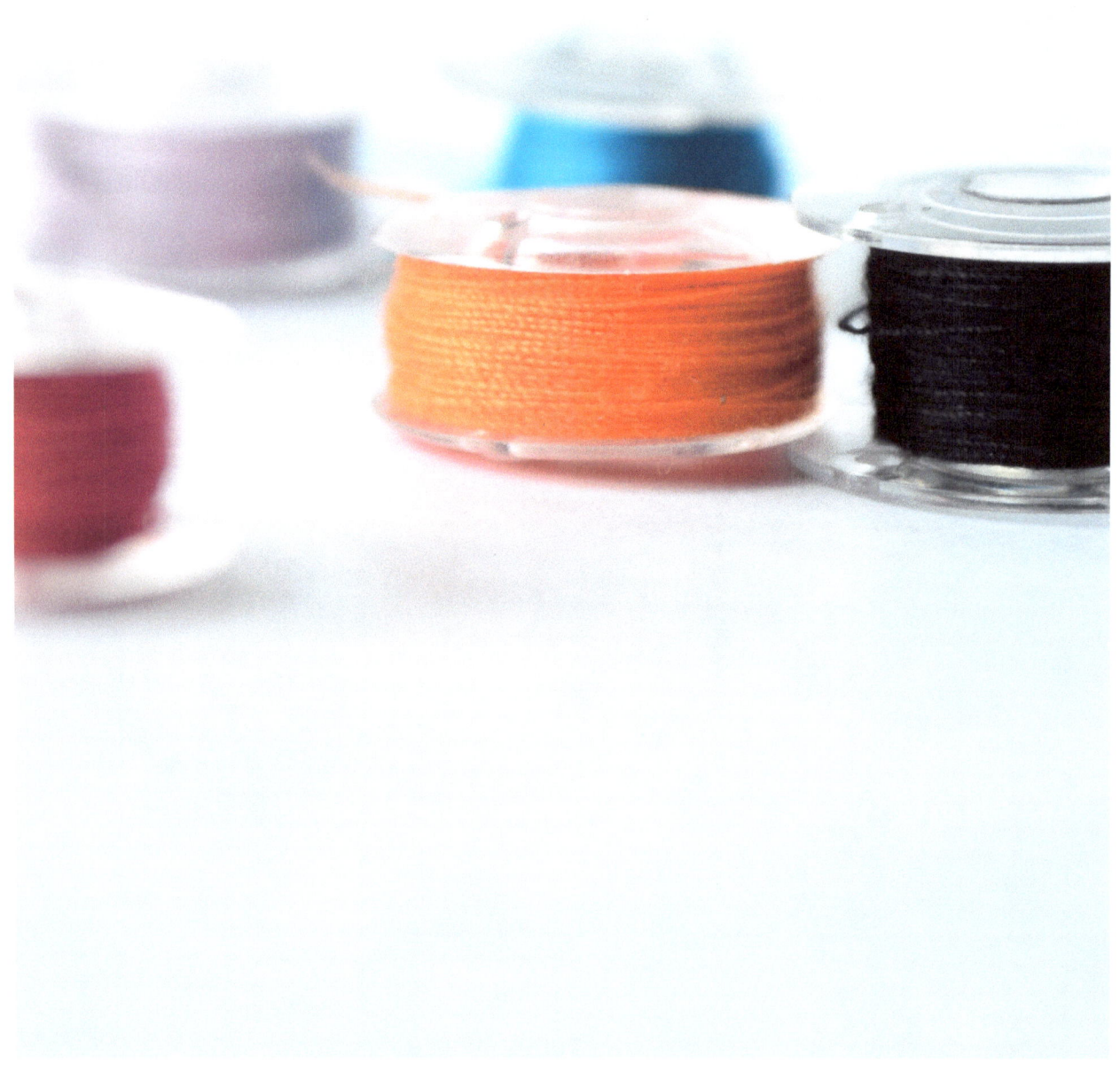

Chapter 8
Finishing Touches

We are now on to the final touches needed for completing your first portrait.

Blocking your Quilt

Pro Tip: Be sure that the fabrics in your quilt are colourfast before blocking. Also, be sure to block the quilt, before binding it.
You will need an area big enough to lay out your quilt to let it dry. This should be an area where pets won't disturb the quilt and no one will walk on the quilt.

Equipment needed:

Surface - When blocking a quilt, there are 3 surface options:

Note: You may only use one of these options, or you may find that you use different options depending on the size of your quilt.

1) Rug (if you have one on the floor) – wall to wall carpet is best, and a space where you can lay out your quilt for some time without anyone walking on it, or in the case of pets, laying on it.

If using your rug to block your quilt, place a sheet on the floor to protect the rug and your quilt.

Or

2) Foam play mats – enough pieces to create a surface larger than your quilt.

For example – in this case, you will only need enough mats to create a space of about 24" x 28" to accommodate your quilt.

As I often create larger quilts, I purchased 2 sets of alphabet mats which had 26 tiles in each set. They came in a plastic zipper case that is great for storing them.

Various mats differ in the size and number of tiles in each package.

Check to see if the number of pieces listed on the package includes only the larger squares, or whether they include the small border pieces in the final count. This is usually easy to see when looking at the picture on the package.

I used these mats on the floor, but they can easily be used on tables.

If you like this idea, I would suggest watching for a sale on these mats.

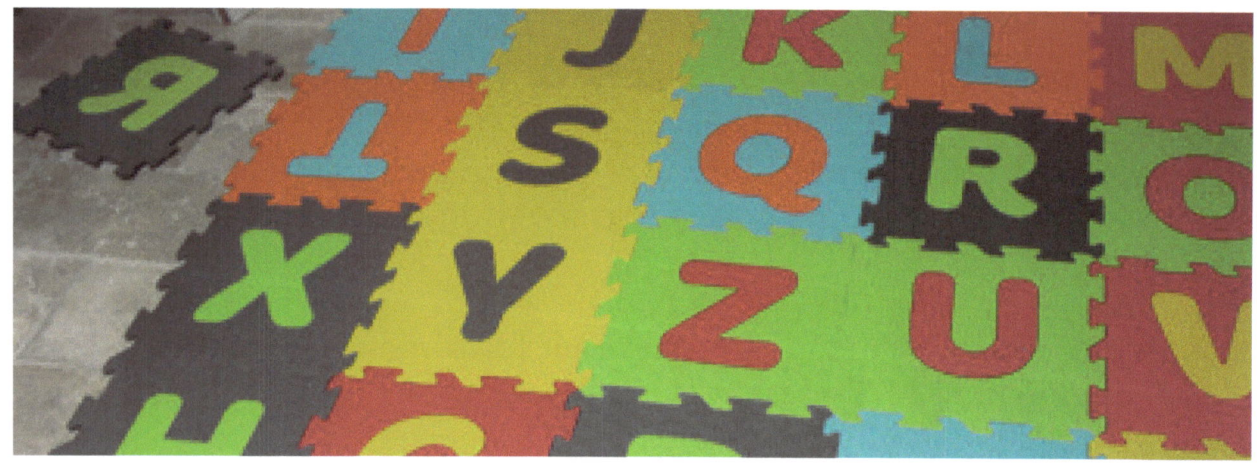

Or

    3) Foam core board– available at Michaels, Walmart or art supply stores.

    You can use the foam board you used as a design wall for this process. Foam boards are great for blocking smaller quilts.

    Depending on how wet your quilt is before blocking, you may need to put a layer of plastic over the foam core before use or it will warp.

Straight pins – lots and lots of them, as you will need to place them about 1 inch apart around the edge of the quilt.

I prefer to use glass headed pins, as I find them easier to handle but any pins will work. I do NOT use my very fine silk pins for this process as they are too delicate.

Rulers – I use both my 12" x 12" large square and my long 6" x 24" rulers.

Tape measure(s) – one that is long enough to measure the length of your quilt and diagonally from corner to corner.

How to Block your quilt

I have used a large quilt of mine to demonstrate this technique.

1. Lay your quilt out on your selected surface smoothing it out.

2. Spray your quilt with water until it is fairly damp.

3. Measure your quilt diagonally from corner to corner, in both directions. These measurements should be the same.

If not, you will need to ease the quilt in, or stretch it out a bit, to get an even measurement.

Stretch carefully, as you don't want to pop any stitches! Pin the corners in place.

4. Now using your large square ruler, start pinning the corner of the quilt putting pins 1" apart. Place the pins so that they are angled out to the outside of the quilt.

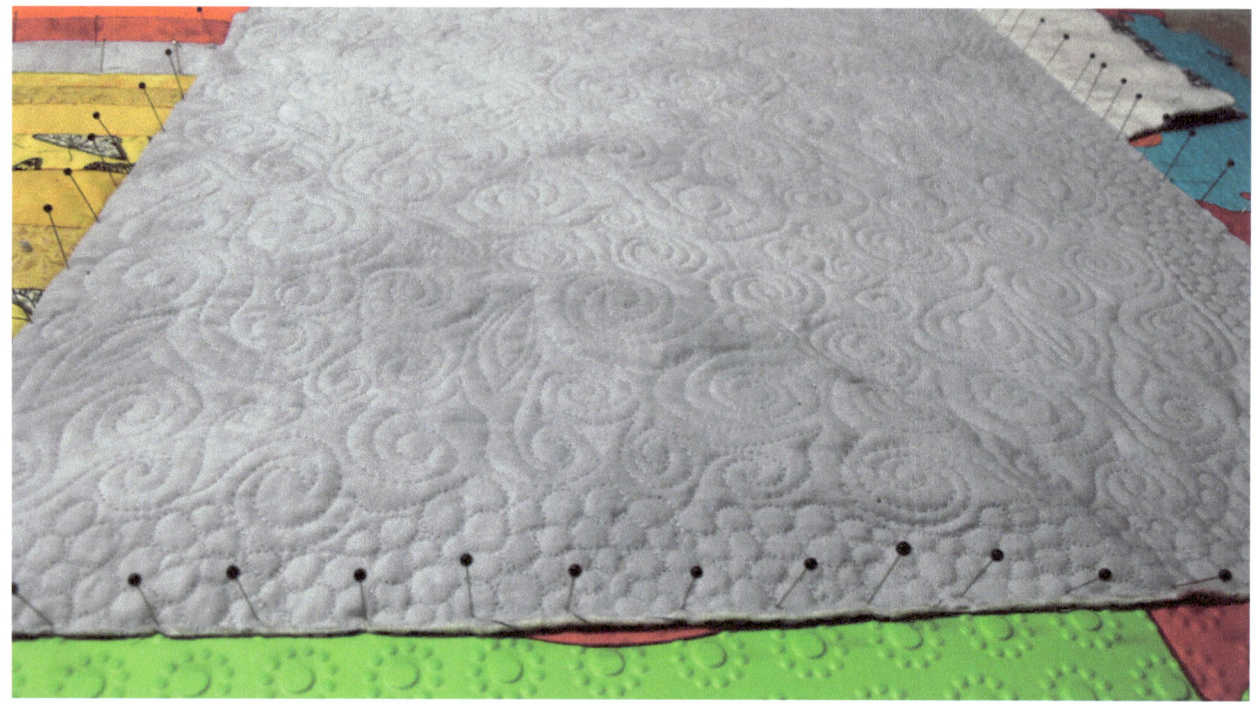

5. Once that is done, gradually straighten the edge of the quilt. There are several ways to do this step:

a) You can use your long ruler placed along the edge of the quilt.
b) A string pulled along the edge of the quilt can help you to see if the edges are straight. You can use a helper for this step or pin the string in place.
c) Some people have found a 90-degree laser level to help with this process of establishing a straight line.

In any case, push and/or pull the edges until they are straight.

6. Now go to the side opposite the one that you just pinned. Using your recorded measurements and a tape measure, adjust your quilt to size and pin it in place starting in the middle and working your way to the corners. Repeat this step with the two other sides working from the middle out to the corners.

7. Once the edges are secure, check the centre of the quilt – is it puffed up at all? If so, it will need to be patted into place.

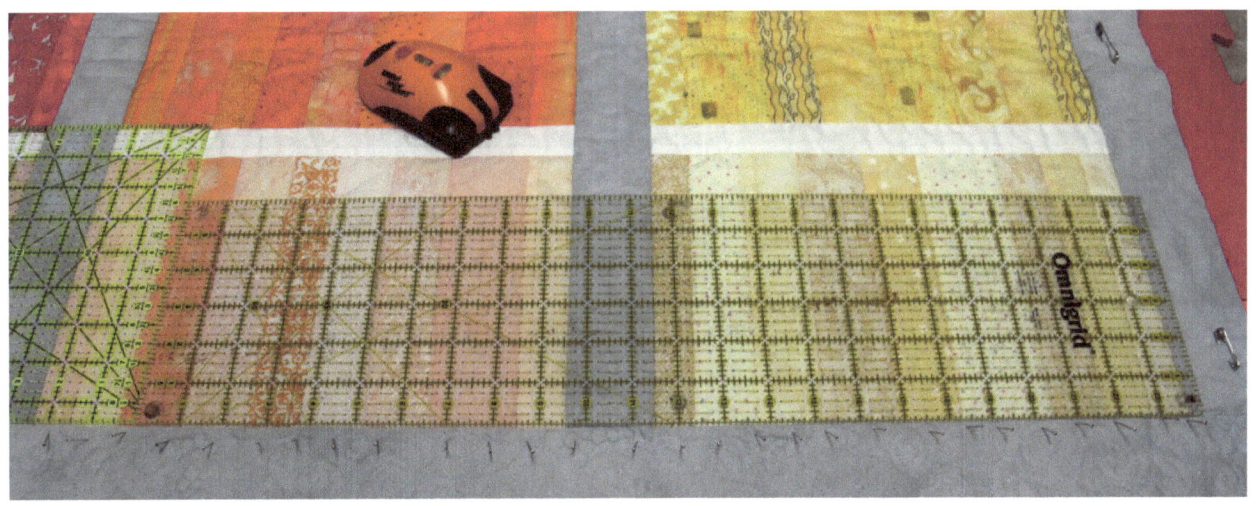

8. Check that the seam line for the border is straight. These lines need to be straight for a great look in your finished quilt.

9. If your weather is very humid, you may want to set up a couple of fans to blow across the surface of the quilt to help it dry.

Let your quilt dry thoroughly. I leave mine for 24 hours.

10. Carefully unpin the edges and enjoy your flat quilt!

11. Slip your cutting mat under the edges of the quilt and use your rulers and rotary cutter to trim the edges.

Pro tip: I use my large square ruler at the corners to make sure that I am keeping the corners square.

Now your quilt is ready for binding or facing. Be careful not to pull the edges of the quilt, when adding the binding!

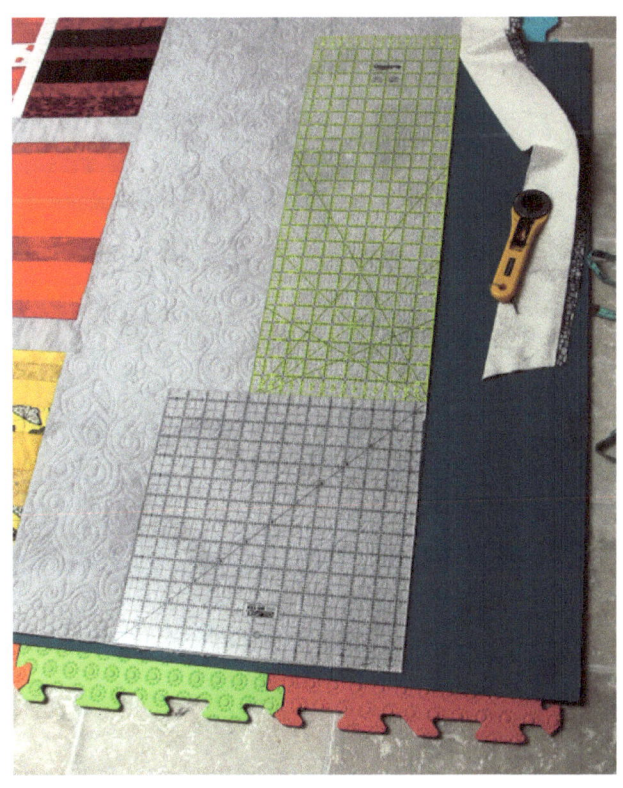

Finishing the Edges

There are a lot of different ways to finish an art quilt. You can zigzag stitch the edge, bind it, use facings or do a pillowcase finish. If you don't already have a favourite finishing technique, search the internet and you will find lots of information on all these techniques.

I use a facing method as I like the clean edge it gives to a quilt. Here is one version of this method. One that I have found particularly easy to do and which gives you great perfectly square corners

Basic Facing

Note: If you are planning on adding facings to your quilt, and it has to finish at a certain size (for example for an exhibit or show), allow an additional 1/2" on all edges of the quilt. This takes into account the seam allowance, the turned edge and rolling the front edge of the quilt to the back.

Note: I used to use a single layer facing to reduce bulk in the seam allowances and corners (as seen in the photos here). Recently I have gone back to a folded facing as I find it easier to handle.

1. Determine the desired width of your facing for the size of the quilt. A smaller quilt will need smaller facings. For this portrait, I used a 2" facing.

2. Assuming a folded facing, and allowing for seam allowances and folding, I would double the size I want my finished facing size to be, plus 1 inch. For example, for a 2-inch facing, I would cut 5-inch strips.

3. Start with the sides of the quilt, measure and cut 2 strips about 1 inch shorter than the length of the side of the quilt. The side facings do not need to reach the corners. Having the side facings shorter means less bulk in the corners.

4. Fold the strips in half lengthwise, with right sides out, and iron them flat.

5. Using a walking foot on your sewing machine, sew the side facings onto the **front** of the quilt, centring them on the sides of the quilt. The walking foot helps to ensure all the layers of the quilt move through the sewing machine at the same rate.

6. Place the facing against the quilt top with the raw edges lined up. See the picture below. In this example, I used facings that were not doubled, but instead only had the edge folded back. The placement is the same.

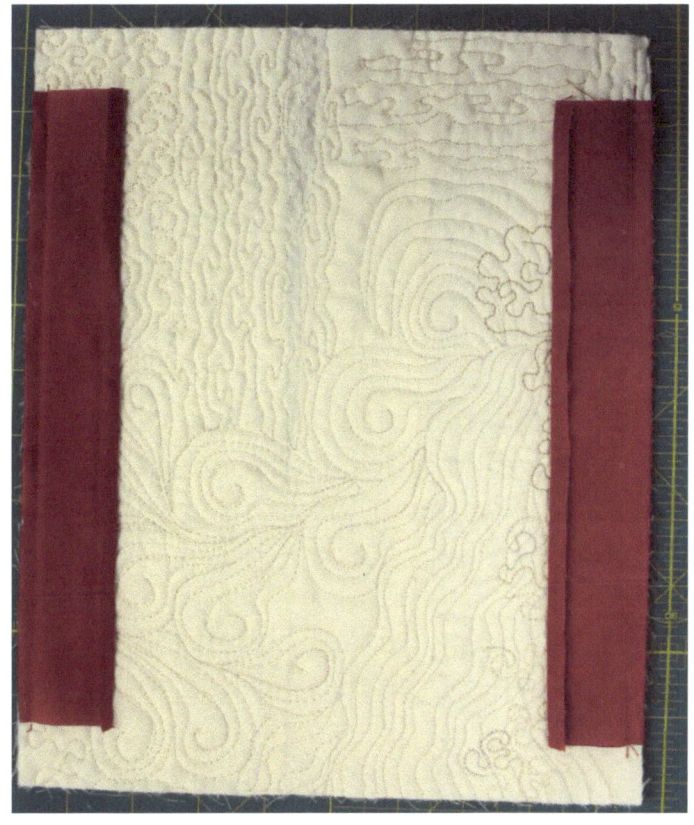

Press the facings outward away from the quilt top and stay stitch through the facing and seam allowance, about 1/16 inch outside the seam line.

Pro Tip: Stay stitching, done with a straight stitch, helps to keep the edge firm and aids in rolling the facing to the back of the quilt.

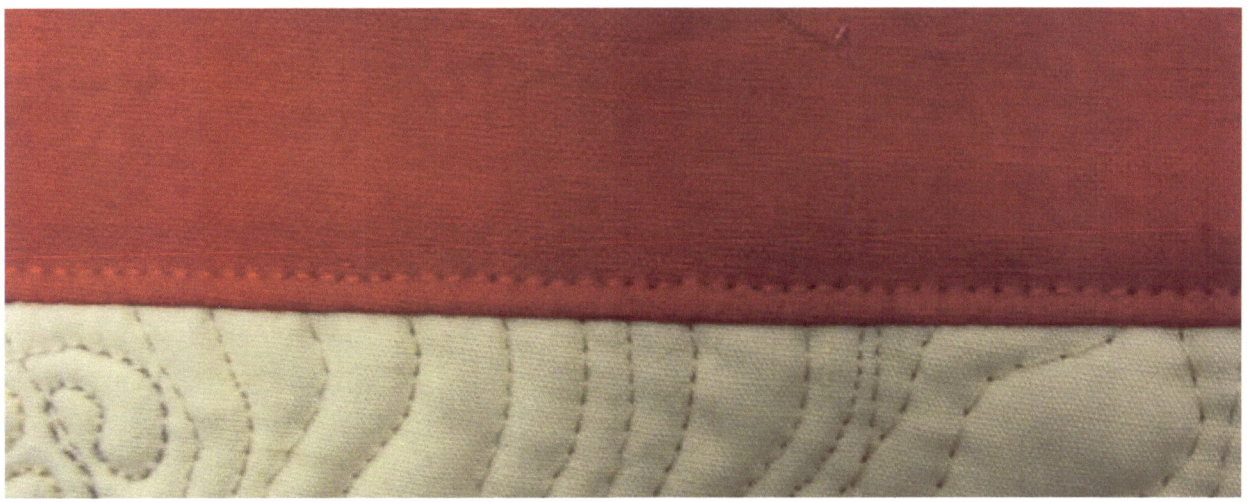

7. Before sewing the top and bottom facings onto the quilt, trim the corners of the batting only at a diagonal approx. 3/8 inch inside the corner.

Before trimming, move the front and back fabrics out of the way.

You may need to pick out any quilting that goes right into the corner before trimming the batting.

I am showing this quilt with a line drawn where the batting was cut.

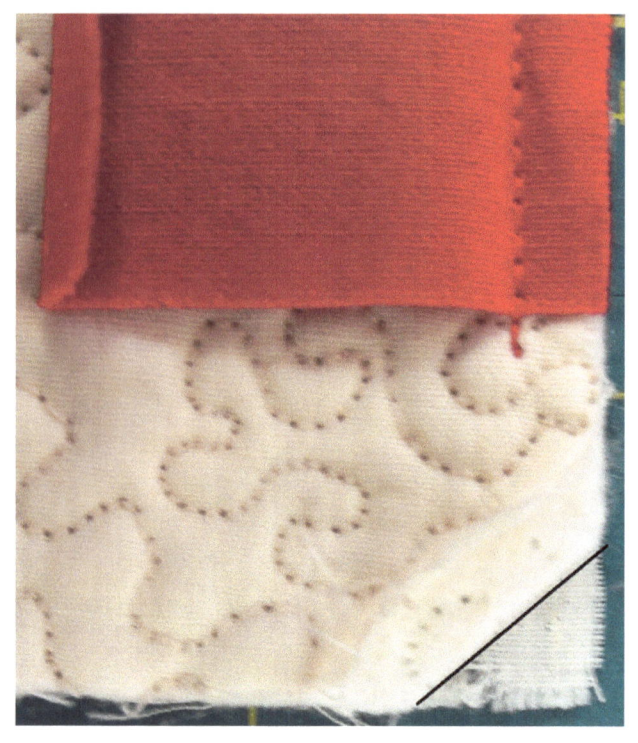

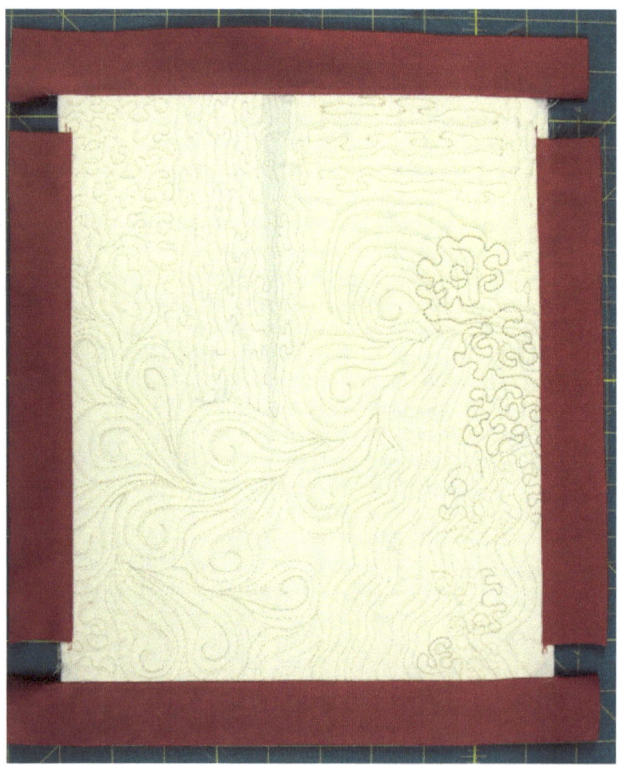

8. For the top and bottom of the quilt, measure and cut 2 facings, each 2 inches longer than the width of the quilt.

9. Sew the top and bottom facings onto the quilt as you did before, allowing an equal amount of overhang at each edge.

10. Press the facings outward.

11. Stay stitch through the facing and seam allowance, about 1/16 of an inch outside the seam line.

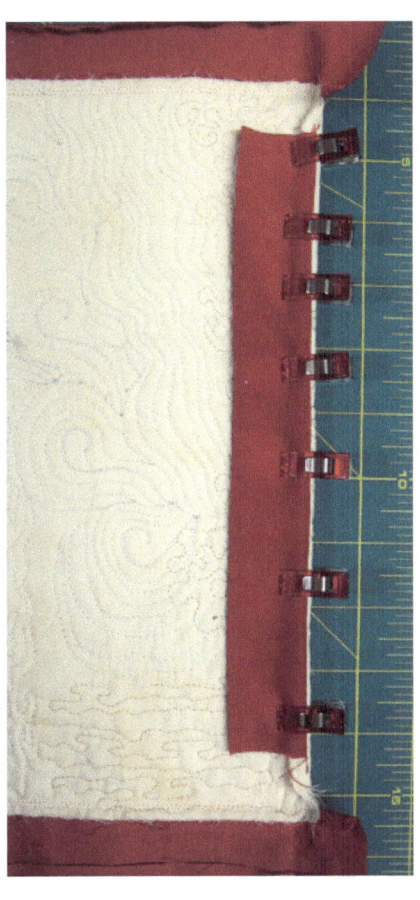

12. Press the **side** facings to the back of the quilt, rolling the edges of the quilt, so that none of the facings shows on the front and a small edge of the front of the quilt shows on the back. Spray with water or use steam to help with this process. Adding the binding clips as you go helps to keep the edge rolled.

13. Sew the folded edge of the side facings down by hand, with a blind stitch. Be careful that you do not stitch through to the front of the quilt.

Pro tip: an alternative to hand sewing the facing is to use ½" Lite Steam-A-Seam 2® (available in rolls) inserted under the edge of the facing. Fuse in place.

14. Fold the top and bottom facings to the back of the quilt, rolling the edge as previously discussed and tucking in the ends of the facing. The ends of the facing can be trimmed to 1/2 of an inch if needed.

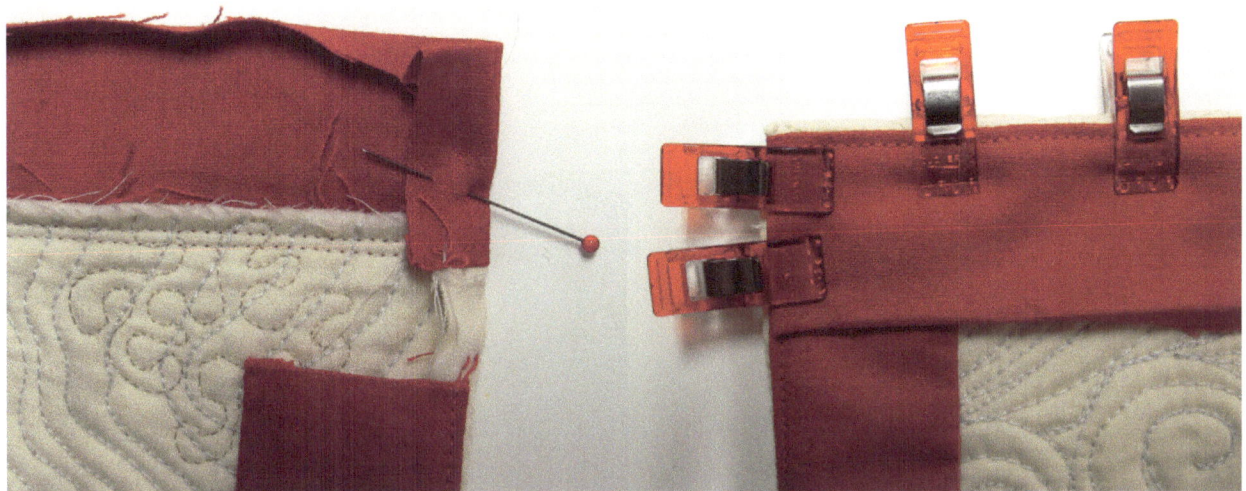

Check that your corners look square from the front as well.

If they do not, refold and press again.

This process may require a little fussing, but you will end up with nice square corners with no lumps.

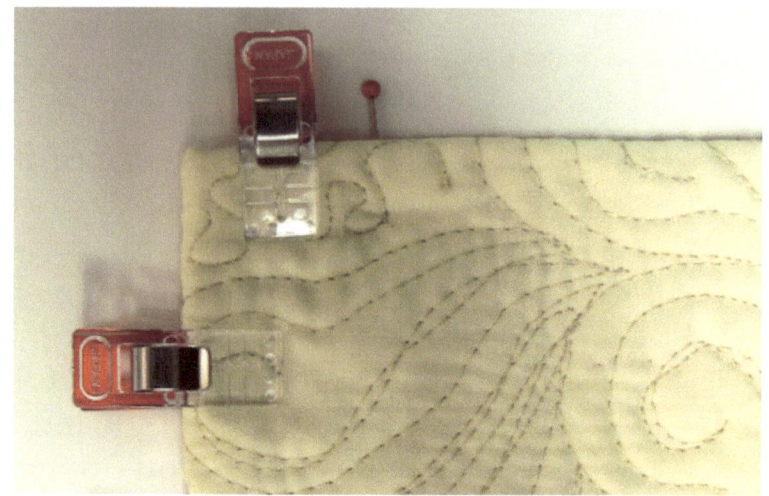

15. Stitch the folded edge of the facings to the back of the quilt with a blind stitch.

Or again use the ½" Lite Steam-A-Seam 2 ®. You will need to put a small piece of the fusible under the folds at the ends to hold them in place, as well as along the edge.

Adding a Hanging Sleeve

There are various ways to hang an art quilt. If you search on the internet for "sleeve for a quilted wall hanging" you will see lots of options.

The most common method, however, is to sew a sleeve to the back of the quilt. This allows for a rod to be put in the sleeve to support the weight of the quilt.

If you use the same fabric as for the backing for your quilt, the sleeve will *disappear*, i.e. blend with the backing fabric.

Creating the sleeve

For this example, I have used a floral fabric as it is easier to see than one that matches the backing of my quilt.

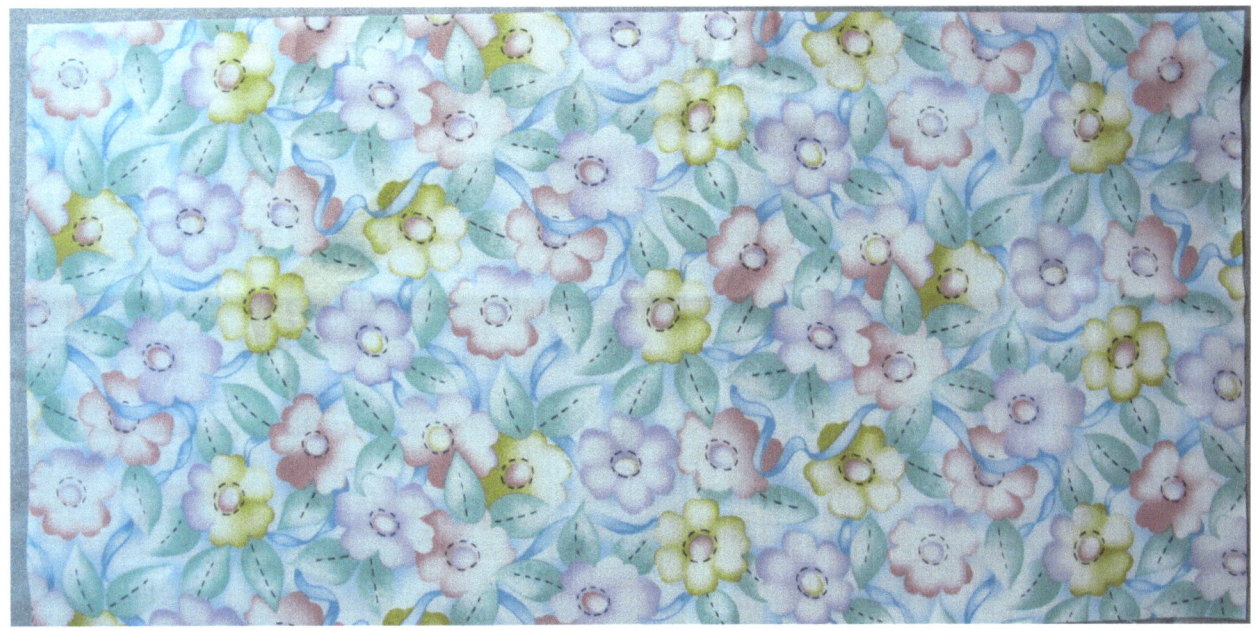

1. Cut a piece of fabric that is one inch shorter than the width of your quilt by 8 ½" wide. This will make a 4" wide sleeve. This is the standard width required for quilt shows.
2. Fold the short ends of the fabric in about ¼" and then fold again tucking the raw edges in.

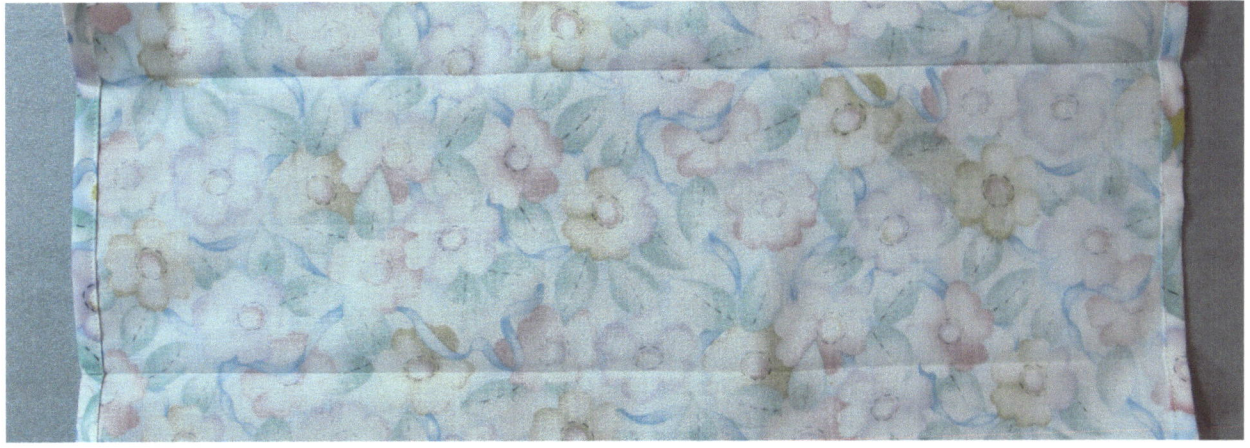

3. Sew the folded edge with a straight or zigzag stitch to secure it in place.
4. Fold the fabric lengthwise, with wrong sides together and finger press the fold.
5. Unfold the fabric and fold each long edge of the fabric to meet at the centre crease. Press with the iron.

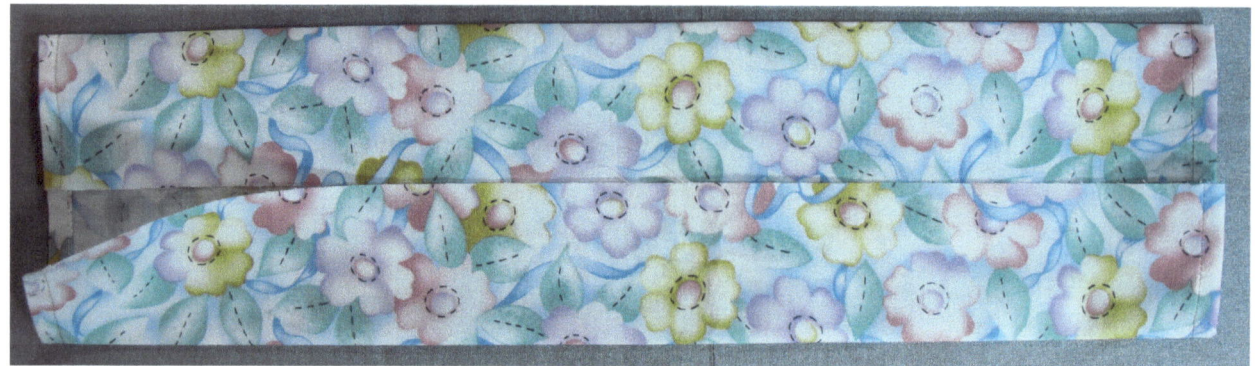

6. Pick the fabric up and pin the long edges together, with wrong sides of the fabric facing each other.

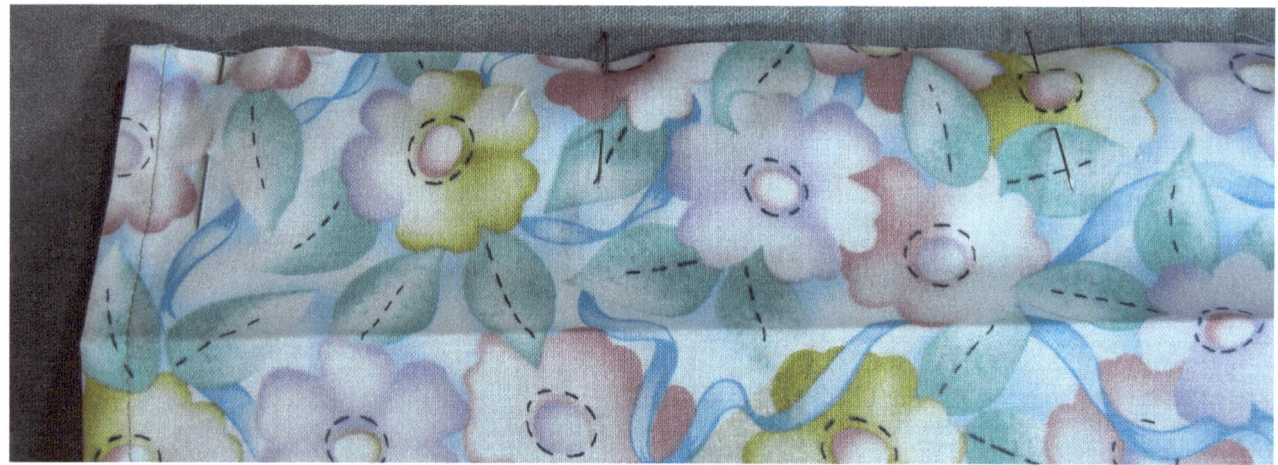

7. Sew the edges together with a ¼" seam. One side of the tube (opposite the seam) will be longer than the other (bulge out) between the folds. This is the way it should be. This slack allows room for the hanging rod.

8. Place the sleeve on the back of your quilt with the seam against the backing of the quilt. Position the sleeve 1" down from the top and centred on the back of the quilt. There should be a bulge in the sleeve. You will be sewing the folded edges to the back of the quilt sandwich.

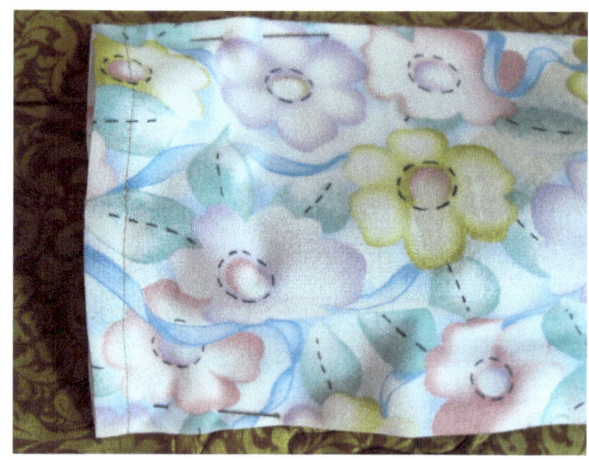

9. Pin the sleeve securely in place. Hand sew the sleeve to the back of the quilt starting with the top edge, being careful to keep it straight and not to sew through to the front of the quilt.

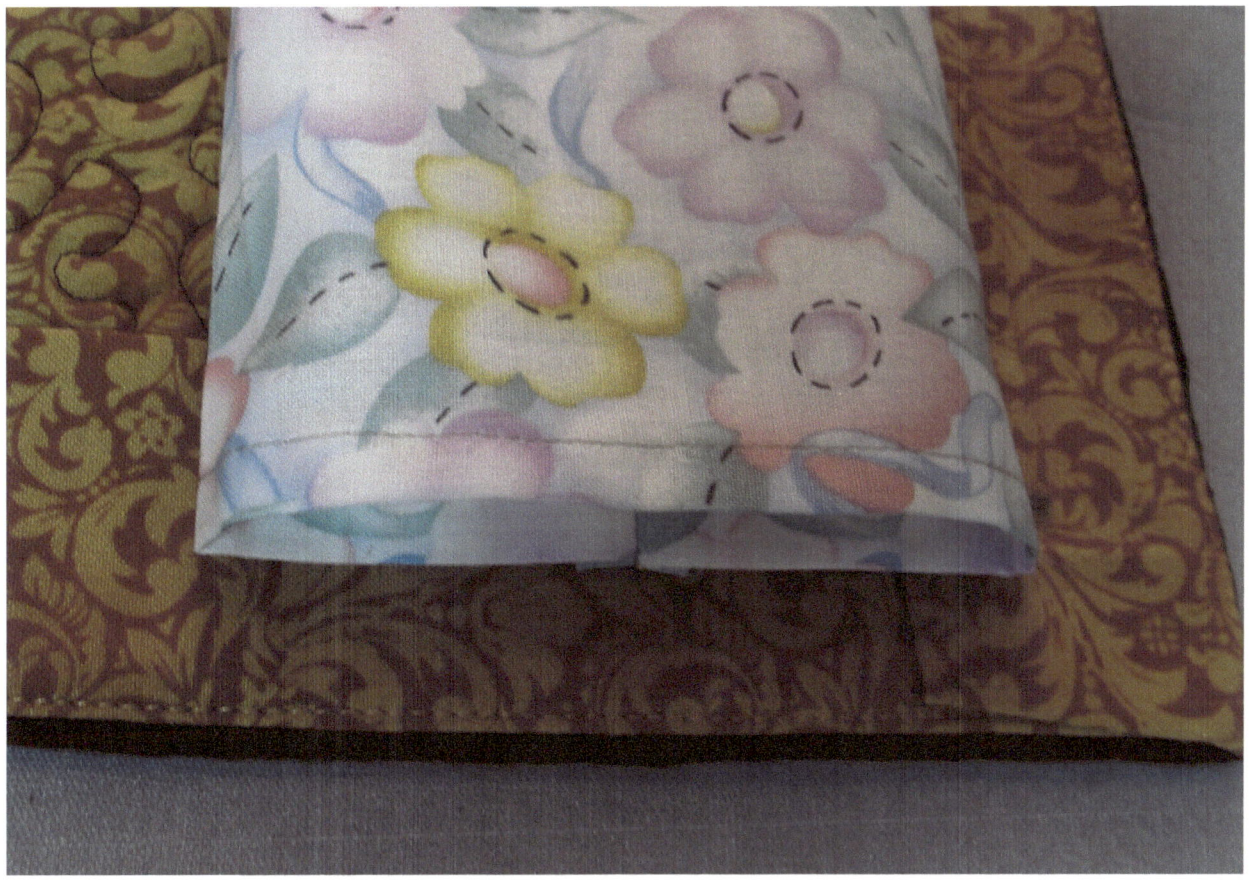

10. Once the top edge is sewn in place, sew down the ends, being careful to keep them lined up parallel to the sides. Make sure that the bottom edge is on the fold. There should be a bulge in the top of the sleeve between the folded edges.

Congratulations! You have finished your portrait!

Letter from the Author

I hope that this book has helped you in your journey into fabric portraits.

Learning is a journey from novice to experienced. Pat yourself on the back for having dared to try something new. Your first portrait is where you become familiar with the technique, gain some skills, and learn what does and does not work. If you decide to continue with this journey, you will find that you get better and better at creating fabric portraits.

Learn to relax and enjoy the process. Once, my mother gave me some advice about wallpapering. She said, "Learn how to correct your mistakes because you are going to make them." It was great advice and applies to quilting as well. This book is only a beginning.

If you would like to learn more about creating fabric portraits, check out my full portraits course, Facial Expressions. I put the link to it, in the resources section at the back of this book. The course covers everything you need to know, to choose your photograph, create a pattern, and even choose the fabric, for creating your family heirloom. Of course, lots of support and encouragement is included.

You can follow me on Facebook at Creating Fibre Art with Valerie Wilson (https://www.facebook.com/ValerieWilsonArtist/)

If you want to learn more about fabric portraits and art quilts, you can sign up for a free newsletter on my website at https://valeriewilsonartist.com or join my Facebook group – Fabric Faces, where we discuss everything about creating fabric portraits.

There are also additional resources at the back of this book.

Thank you for taking this journey with me. I appreciate your interest and wish you all the best on your journey.

Valerie Wilson - Fibre Artist

Your Resources

Chapter 1
Sources for Mylar (Dura-Lar)
try art supply stores but there are also these online suppliers:

- Dick Blick Art Materials - U.S.
    - https://www.dickblick.com

- Opus Art Supplies - Canada
    - Opusartsupplies.com

- Swift Supplies - Australia
    - https://www.swiftsupplies.com.au/polyester-film-sheet

Chapter 2
 Gray scale – artisticquilts.net

Chapter 3
Skin tone fabrics
- hand-dyed - artisticquilts.net
- kit for the class artisticquilts.net

Chapter 5
Top 10 Tips for using Lite Steam-A-Seam 2 ®
- https://valeriewilsonartist.com/steam-a-seam-ii-lite-top-10-tips-for-success/

Chapter 6
Article on thread weights
- https://www.superiorthreads/education/thread-weight

Needle types and sizes
- https://www.superiorthreads.com/education/needle-guide

Chapter 7
Book - Walking Foot Quilting Designs:
- https://marginet.weebly.com/my-books.html

Chapter 8
Sewing a hanging sleeve for a quilt
- https://mulberrypatchquilts.wordpress.com/2018/06/29/how-to-hang-a-quilt-on-the-wall/

Letter from the Author
Fabric portraits workshop:
- https://www.valeriewilsonartist.net

Fabric Faces Facebook group:
- https://www.facebook.com/groups/fabricfaces

My web site:
- https://valeriewilsonartist.com

Facebook page:
- https://www.facebook.com/ValerieWilsonArtist

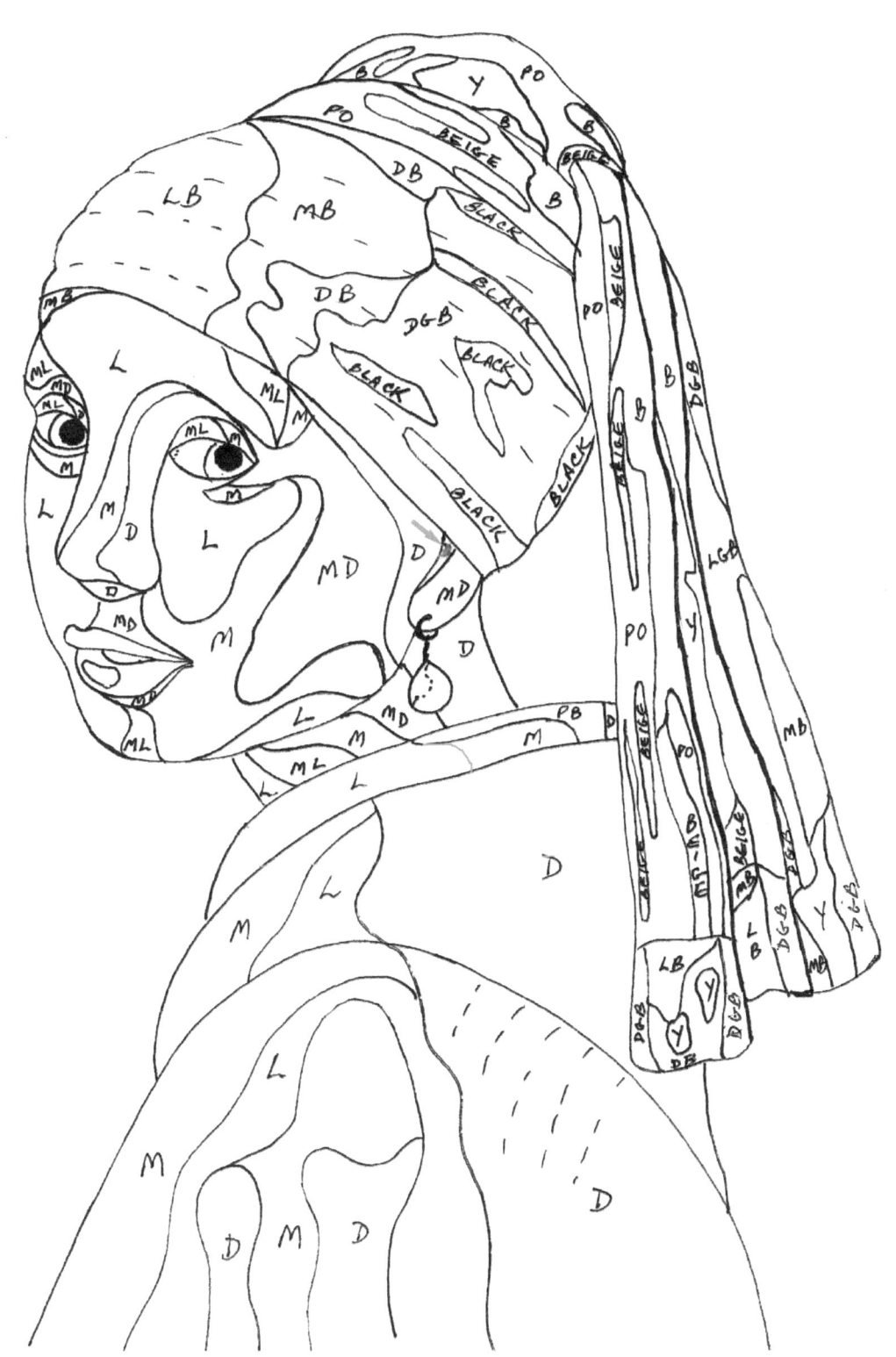

www.ingramcontent.com/pod-product-compliance
Lightning Source LLC
Chambersburg PA
CBHW051912210526
45473CB00006B/1990